Dreams

. . . .

Mirrors of Your Soul

Dreams

· · · · · · ·

Mirrors of Your Soul

MARIE FRIEND

TURNING
STONE
PRESS

First published in 2015 by
Turning Stone Press, an imprint of
Red Wheel/Weiser, LLC
With offices at:
665 Third Street, Suite 400
San Francisco, CA 94107
www.redwheelweiser.com

ISBN: 978-1-61852-092-0

Cover design by Jim Warner
Cover image: © Triff / shutterstock
© Lambros Kazan / shutterstock

Printed in the United States of America
10 9 8 7 6 5 4 3 2 1

Table of Contents

To every Soul who has dared to dream.

Acknowledgments

Saying "thank you" to all the people who contributed to the making of this book seems so inadequate. How can those two simple words convey my humble appreciation of those who selflessly gave of themselves when I asked for help—even without any expectations of getting something in return?

Among many of these like-minded souls, Kathy Holtby is one of those who trusted and accepted my delving into her most inner psyche. She not only allowed me into her most personal sub-conscious but also offered her beautiful spirit as a friend. Likewise, my gratitude will remain for Marie Jackson: another sensitive human who knows that she is still first and foremost a spirit experiencing humanity's strengths and weaknesses. Although Madge Peinkofer doesn't realize it, her profound gifts of oration, when listening to her sermons, influenced many of my thoughts while writing *Dreams, Mirrors of Your Soul*.

Without a doubt this book would be just another dream book if it was not for the generosity of those amazing folks who responded to my request to share their dreams with me. Without any reticence, they shared their deepest uncertainties, fears, and foibles that came forth from their deep rooted pyches. They openly shared with me their fascinating life stories via their dreams. My email was overwhelmed with responses to this request and my only regret is that it was impossible to share all of them within these pages. Regardless, my heartfelt thanks are extended to all those people who shared their dreams with me. I'm reminded of the saying "The teacher learns from the student" and yours truly feels like their assistance has helped me to pass the test of knowledge with this book!

Last but certainly not least I extend a warm and grateful thank you to all the people at my publishing house. At the risk of sounding like a repetitive Oscar Award recipient I have to say that without them this book wouldn't have been possible.

Namaste.

Alternate realities

Existing, intermingling, remote

Clay before the firing

Solidified in the moment

and experienced.

—Cassandra

⚮ 1 ⚭

Introduction to
Your Subconscious

A re you one of those people who will confidently state that you never dream? Ah, you're so wrong. Of course you do! Everyone does. The fact is that some people just don't remember and you could be one of those people. That's probably the reason why you picked this book up in the first place—because whether you realize it or not, your subconscious is prodding you into learning more about how dreams work in your life and what those dreams mean to you. Dreams are a great tool to use when you want to know what really makes you tick. And, by the time you've come to the last page—well, I guarantee that at least you'll have learned how important dreams are to your life. At the most you will have uncovered how to read the messages that your dreams bring to you.

Before we start, let me explain a little bit about myself and why I feel qualified to present this system of dream analysis to you. I'm a "show me" type of individual and therefore feel that everyone should be given tangible proof of anything metaphysical or paranormal. I most firmly believe that everyone has the right to have their own spirituality validated. Everyone deserves to know their own Self. In other words, I don't rely completely on faith. Because I have respect for any person seeking answers to their metaphysical or spiritual questions, I don't just say, "If you don't believe it, just listen to me." If I can't provide a proof in response to a question, I'll say so and then assist in finding the answer that person is seeking. The payback for following this philosophy is that I learn something new in the process of finding the answer! Like the biblical adage states, "Seek, and you will find; knock, and it will be opened unto you." It can't get much clearer than that.

My maternal great grandparents were Welsh gypsies, and my mother was psychic even though she never practiced outside the family. Some of my earliest memories are of attending Spiritualist churches with my mother and an aunt who shared the same ancestry. As far back as I can remember I have experienced precognitive dreams, and I grew up thinking that everyone did because my mother and her clan all took this phenomenon as a matter of fact.

As a child I chose to attend Sunday school only when I felt like it and, unlike many of my friends, was not forced by my parents into showing up every Sabbath. In other words, I was taught at an early age to think for myself. I often questioned fundamental religious doctrines before they were instilled into my young mind. Logic told me that there had to be more to certain stories than what the church Sunday school told me to believe. Were these biblical tales absolute fact? Some sounded so far-fetched that my childish mind believed them to be fairy tales. For example, I remember as a young teenager asking a question of a minister who gave me the answer that "You have to take it on faith." Instinctively I realized that he didn't have the answer, and my estimation of him took a decided plummet. I wondered why he couldn't be honest and just say, "I don't know the answer to that." No doubt being a cleric it was second nature for him to rely on faith for everything concerning his religious beliefs, and a child should not have the audacity to question the validity of the Bible stories. But for the young, curious person that I was, his answer seemed like a cop-out. Fortunately, with more adult experiences behind me I can look back on his answer and realize that we all have our own Truth. He was being honest unto himself. His faith in his personal beliefs was unshakable, and he couldn't possibly fathom a young mind that needed logical explanations.

Regardless of my skepticism and the fact that I still ask for logical solutions to my questions, I've never questioned my belief in the importance of dreams. All my life I've had precognitive dreams, and because of this, I take my dream-time as seriously as I take control of my life. This is one area of Self that I don't question or ask for proof about, because it's been given to me too many times to count. Hence, this book is a culmination of a lifetime spent acknowledging the veracity of dream messages. My intent, dear reader, is to share with you what I've learned, in the hope that it will provide answers to your own questions concerning your dreams in relationship to your path in life.

The major intent of *Dreams: Mirrors of Your Soul* is to open your mind to a deeper knowledge of *who you are* beyond your physical persona. Dreaming is just one method whereby we're given the tools to use our subconscious to guide our conscious mind. We are more than just a body with a mind that helps us to function. *We are Spirit having a human experience.* Neglecting to utilize the wisdom of that spirit is like a right-handed individual trying to write with the left hand. You may be able to make your signature with the left hand, but it is more than likely to be as illegible as a doctor's script on a prescription. Just as your fingerprints are unique, so are you. In other words, you are more than just another face in the crowd.

Most people have become so used to operating in our so-called civilized world that we've forgotten how to function as a whole being. The dream-state is just one aspect of the expanded knowledge about yourself that your subconscious can provide—if you allow it to. Your subconscious has many functions, but I'm going to cover one aspect only of its reasoning: its function for the dreamer. This book will give you a good start so that you can "write" with your left hand (subconscious brain) and be able to consciously decipher what you've written. Through listening to and understanding your dreams you will be able to absorb the deeper meaning of who you are. The purpose of this book is not only for you to realize that in fact you really do dream, but more important, it's designed to show you how to use the messages that dreams bring to you to help make your daily life easier. Learning to understand your dreams can be an important helpmate in applying your everyday decision making.

Following your dreams' guidance can steer you right with anything that you need to know, such as about relationship problems that may be troubling you, money matters, health situations, your working environment, and any other subject that crops up whereby you need to make an important choice. Who wouldn't like to have an easy road to walk through life rather than running the risk of stumbling and falling into a ravine or feeling your way blindly through dark caves?

Understanding your dreams won't guarantee that life's challenges will be a breeze, but at least they'll tell you how to travel carefully through tricky situations and be alert to approaching storms. By listening to the messages of your dreams and exploring their wisdom, you can navigate through some of the pitfalls of life and avoid unhappy outcomes resulting from wrong decision making. Believe me, your dream-stories can help you to heal many things that might be hampering your potential— if you will only let them. All you have to do is to take heed and listen to your dreams' messages. Think of this book as a "foreign language" text that you're studying. *Dreams: Mirrors of The Soul* is designed for you to explore the foreign language of dreams in an intelligible way. Alongside a foreign word is the equivalent in your own familiar language.

I can't emphasize enough how important dreams are in all of our lives. They're as necessary as taking in deep breaths of oxygen and exhaling poisonous carbon dioxide. Ignoring the message that a dream is bringing to you is a hindrance to your overall well-being because whether you are consciously aware of them or not, dreams are an essential part of your life. And yes, they're as important to you as breathing in fresh air.

We are fortunate to live in an era when not only the metaphysically minded public is beginning to realize the importance of dreams but the scientific community has also become more open to their impact. This is especially true since those well-known psychologists Sigmund Freud and Carl Jung publicly and dramatically threw open the door to the realm of dreams as a form of healing for the psyche. Scientists have coined the term *oneirology* to describe the study of dreams, and they take these studies very seriously, albeit from a scientific perspective. What is so exciting about this age we are living in is that the gap between quantum physics and metaphysics is closing. Not only are we humans exploring outer space, but we're delving into our own inner space. This has never been more true than it is with the dream-world.

For example, scientific studies have found a correlation between the use of hallucinogenic drugs and their impact on a person's dreams. Apparently these drugs can enhance and exacerbate one's dreams. But, never having taken any such drugs (I'm a devout coward and need to have more control over my mind), I can only take scientists' word for this. It has also been found that certain prescription drugs can have an effect on the type of dreams a person experiences. This shouldn't be a surprise to anybody, as any drug is capable of altering body chemistry. A movie some years ago called *Flatliners* starring Keifer Sutherland explored interesting examples of manipulating the brain to produce altered states of consciousness and out-of-body experiences via dreams. It is well worth watching.

However, scientists who have studied dreams via experimentation will agree that working under such controlled environments is very difficult to do. Obviously the dream-state is a complete contrast to the waking state, so consideration of the dreamer's mental attitude during sleep has to be taken into account. It is possible for a scientist to perform what is called a "contact analysis" of a dream, but even in this state the scientist still has to interpret the symbols of the dream and their meaning by taking into consideration the sleeping person's state of mind. What has been happening in the dreamer's life that day or how are they feeling about certain things in their everyday life? What message is the subconscious attempting to bring to the forefront of this person's mind? Inevitably this brings us back to where we started: metaphysical concepts.

If you desire to learn more about dreams from a scientific point of view, you will find plenty of interesting books dealing with this specific subject. But, as my intent is to help those readers who are interested in using their dreams as an aid in their everyday activities, I'm going to leave the science of dreams to those with more expertise than yours truly. The bottom line is that dreams occur for a specific reason and are telling it to you "like it is." Whether you choose to use them to help you in your daily decision making is entirely up to you.

Even if you claim to not have dreams, the subconscious is still operating to produce them. Picture yourself working on a factory assembly line and you're placing parts together on a moving belt in order to make a workable object. You've been doing this for so long, day in and day out, that you automatically perform your task by rote. Even though your thoughts may be elsewhere, such as what you did the evening before or what you plan to fix for dinner when you return home, you are still automatically assembling the parts correctly into a usable object. You have done the same thing so often on a daily basis, that it's as if you're on autopilot. That's exactly how your subconscious works when you are asleep. You may not be remembering your dreams, but that doesn't stop the "conveyer belt" from delivering the nuts and bolts to your psyche so that you can "assemble" them into a helpful message.

While you are sleeping, your subconscious stays very much awake and is hard at work. There is an old saying that "the mirror doesn't lie," and this is so very true when looking at the mirror of your dreams. Contemplate for a moment the fairy stories of your childhood. For example, there's a subtle message that exists in the tale of Snow White and her wicked stepmother. The stepmother asks her magic mirror if she is the fairest in all the land. Remember the mirror's answer? "No." Snow White is more beautiful, of course. The stepmother doesn't like the answer, but the mirror can't lie. There is much more than just a childish story to most fairy tales. Dreams can't lie. It's as if you were holding a mirror in front of your face and seeing who you really are without any guile or pretense. A mirror forces you to look at the *real* you; so do your dreams. Your subconscious is without any subterfuge so it brings forth all the warts as well as beauty spots that everyone has and reveals them to you through psychological stories.

Another fairy-tale writer, namely Hans Christian Andersen, was also a great teacher of Life. Really dissect his story of "The Emperor's New Clothes." Know the one? Of course you do! Everyone was afraid to tell this king that he was as naked as a jaybird. And so, what did they do? They complimented him on his new outfit even though he wasn't wearing anything but his birthday suit, that is, until a person came along who had the nerve to speak the truth. Your well-meaning family and friends may tell you what you want to hear about yourself, but your dreams see you as naked as the day you were born. Your dreams tell the truth, whether you like it or not.

You need to think of your dreams as being your own personal truth-teller bringing you many different facets of your own Self. You and I are going to explore all those facets. Together we'll cover dreams with regard to everything that may be happening to you in your waking life. Everything that is impacting your body, mind, and spirit is covered via dreams. They bring into your consciousness every detail of your waking experiences and will even give you clues as to why you are here again, by showing you past-life scenarios that may be impacting this life's journey. Just as we create our own waking reality, we create our own dream-world through our subconsciousness memories.

So before we start, let's get down to the basics of dreams. You probably know that dreams take place during the REM (rapid eye movement) stages of sleep. The body is immobile during REM sleep, and this is when your subconscious brain is activated to help your memory and learning processes. Interestingly, it's been found that infants spend approximately 50 percent of their sleep in the REM stage, whereas an adult spends only 20 percent. One theory that's been put forth is that this accounts for an infant's rapid capacity for learning during infancy that begins with all the development taking place within the first two years of his/her life, such as crawling, walking, and talking.

In contrast, it has been proven that people who are deprived of sleep suffer memory loss and other debilitating mental ailments. Remember how you felt that morning after you had a lousy night's sleep? Ugh! A stark example of the dangers of sleep deprivation is the captive soldier who is deliberately not allowed to sleep as a means of torture. It's this REM stage of sleep that we need.

Apparently we experience several phases of this lighter sleep-time during the night, but usually it's toward morning that we recall our dreams most clearly. Yet, sometimes during the night, if we awaken after experiencing a

REM stage of sleep, we may recall a dream quite vividly, especially if it's a nightmare. Believe it or not, even the latter have their uses, but we'll get into the subject of nightmares later.

So, how do you actively engage with all this sleep-time brain activity that is going on whether you are aware of it or not? If you seriously want to remember your dreams, a good place to start is to *simply believe that you can*. Negative thoughts have their own dynamic. Words such as "I never remember my dreams" are energetic, and your subconscious will pick up your intent and act accordingly. Say anything often enough and you'll finally convince yourself that it's true. Instead, try thinking or saying something positive like "I know I can remember my dreams" or "I'm open to receiving and understanding the messages of my dreams." What you think, you are. *You* control your mind: it doesn't control you—unless you allow it to.

Make a point of relaxing completely before going to bed.

Watching a scary movie and/or eating junk food won't cut it! Eat healthily. Save the horror flicks, popcorn, so-called "energy" drinks, and potato chips for another time. Most healthy diets urge you to drink plenty of water, but even so, don't drink too much before going to bed. You'll interrupt your dreams with too many visits to the bath-room. Personally, I drink plenty of fluids during the day but stop before eight o'clock at night.

Write down your requests and intentions.

This is for benefit of your conscious brain. Your subconscious is already standing by to accommodate your intent.

If you are having a problem that is nagging at you and you don't know how to solve it, ask for help. I do.

When I've explored all the options I can think of for resolving the problem and even my gut instincts have drawn a blank, I turn to my dreams. Once I *let go* (two magic words) and turn it over to my Inner Guidance—better known as the subconscious—I'll invariably get the answer to the problem via a dream, or at the very least, I'll awaken knowing the answer. It's that simple. Life itself is really simple. It's we humans that make it so complicated. Write down affirmations of your needs.

Reading affirmations or saying them out loud will condition your mind and point it in the right direction. It's easier than you think. I write favorite affirmations on cards and place them in spots where my eyes automatically take them in, such as the bathroom mirror and over my car visor, even on my computer. If you have one of those sophisticated, newfangled cell phones or other electronic contraptions, enter an affirmation that will pop up and catch your eye as you open it up to use. Change the affirmation periodically so it won't grow stale.

It may take a few times of diligent working to recall your dreams in order for your subconscious to get well oiled and begin functioning on all cylinders. Be patient. Ignoring your dreams for most of your life is the same as if you neglected your car. If you don't put oil in your car or change it when needed, the car will eventually develop problems or stop running altogether. Neglect maintenance long enough and the engine will eventually freeze up and quit working. It's the same with your subconscious. Treat your subconscious with respect, and it will take care of your welfare.

Do you know that there is a part of our brain that is claimed to be of unknown use? At least, that's what psychologists affirm. But I'm convinced otherwise from personal experience. I believe that this uncharted section of our brain is very much alive with unseen dynamic energy. This is where we store all our past memories, not only from the day we were born but also from past lives. I would go so far as to say that this part of the brain is more active than the conscious brain, at least when it comes to minute details.

It used to be a common theory that we spend approximately ninety minutes a night dreaming while we are asleep. In recent years, that theory has changed as exploration into the field of dreaming has become more sophisticated. One dream may seem to last all night. In reality it can vary from minutes to hours. Regardless of how long a dream lasts, our subconscious is inundating us with teaching "stories." In fact, it probably works harder while you're sleeping than you do during an eight-hour workday.

The answer to remembering your dreams is simple. Change your "stinking thinking." *Believing* that you dream is the first step. Learning to interpret your dreams is the fun part. So, now that you have an idea that dreams are not just silly imaginings that your brain conjures up while you are enjoying your slumbers, let's explore further. Let's take a look at the various types of dreams that come to you.

2

Flights of Fancy

Ah! Those flights of freedom to infinite spirituality. They are one of the most enjoyable experiences in this life, and lucky is the person who experiences what is known as astral flying within the limited dimensions of our world. Sometimes during sleep the spirit travels to other worlds. I call these awesome flights into other realities my spiritual sojourns in "Never Never Land."

Most people have felt this at least once, even if they weren't aware of what they were doing. Even those of you who claim not to have dreams or can't remember them have at least once experienced astral flying. You may not have a conscious understanding or memory of what you are doing, but you can't forget the complete feeling of Oneness with your own Divinity. After a night of astral flying one will awaken to a sense of complete tranquility. Children are more apt to experience astral travel while sleeping, probably because their young minds are so fearless and uncluttered by the responsibilities of the adult world.

When I was a child, it was quite common for me to fly like a bird to anyplace I wanted to go to while my body slumbered. Of course, the child that I was didn't know what she was doing, but she also didn't care. I was enjoying the ride! I was as free and as light as the wind, and my spirit soared effortlessly to the heights of the tallest mountain and beyond. Sadly as I've become an adult these spirit flights while sleeping have become a rarity. The innocence of childhood has given way to the responsibilities of this adult life. Lucky is the adult who still experiences the astral fights of their youth. The residue of that nighttime journey into weightlessness lasts throughout your waking day and makes everything you do feel better. It's similar to lucid dreaming, and may even include same, but we'll cover lucid dreams in a later chapter.

Interestingly, I recently dreamed that I was astral flying again, but it wasn't quite as free and effortless as when I was a youngster. In this dream I was piloting a small airplane. Astral flying usually doesn't involve anything beyond your own power, but this time I actually was the plane. My "wings" were having difficulty becoming airborne, yet at the same time that I had misgivings, I was elated at the thought of flying again, even though I was also conscious of the fact that I wasn't sure that I could become free of my body to do so. In my sleeping state I willed myself to fly and thought, "Come on! You can still do this!" It must have been a similar sensation for the Wright brothers as they attempted to get their plane off the ground! Finally I took off, but because of my adult insecurities, I was limited to coasting just a few feet above the earth. Even so, I was once again enjoying the sensation after not having flown in such a long time. My freed spirit traveled a short distance above the land. Eventually I came close to a large lake. My thoughts suddenly became less joyful, and a sense of responsibility set in. I thought I'd better not land in the lake or else I'd be done for! When I landed on what I thought to be solid ground, I found myself mired instead in slushy mud that was part of the lake. Still, I wasn't afraid. It felt familiar to me. Turning over onto my back, I "swam" with a backstroke to get out of the slush.

This dream was a reminder to me that sometimes it's easier to allow oneself to float and "go with the flow" rather than get "swamped" in the responsibilities of life. Every now and again we all need to be aware of the need to "take time to smell the roses." I never did reach the safety of solid land, but it wasn't necessary. I knew that I'd once again had a brief taste of what it was like to be "out there" unencumbered by responsibilities (slushy mud). I had taking a rest on the "Lake of Tranquility" before returning to the usual, heavy duties of life here on earth. But, most important, the astral flight had left me with a sense of peace and lightness that stayed with me for hours. This latter is the true gift one receives from a flight of fancy.

Flights of the spirit are remembered as dreams; however, they're not really dreams but rather an actual freeing of the spirit that we experience while the body is in slumber. And, because your spirit is free, you may communicate quite naturally with your subconscious. It's the same profound spiritual freedom that you may have felt as you watched the kid in the *E.T.* movie as he became airborne while riding his bicycle. Through the genius of Spielberg's imagination, the audience was lifting off with him as he swept past the moon with the alien sitting on his handlebars. If you've watched this movie (and who hasn't), surely that one scene alone captured your sense of awe and remembrance of who you really are: the unlimited power of Spirit.

The difference between *E.T.* and your life is that your astral flight is more personal and you don't need a bike or an alien to get there. What an experience! It's the same feeling of returning to a beloved place that you've visited in the past and getting that wave of nostalgic warmth again. It's better than taking a break from work and enjoying the relaxation found on a sunny beach. The wonderful thing is that, while astral flying, you have the opportunity to receive profound insights into questions you may have about your spiritual and psychological makeup. During these flights, your spirit can travel to anyplace in the Universe and receive awesome knowledge that will manifest in your waking life. So, how do you get to that state of awareness that allows you to leave your body while sleeping and to consciously know what you are doing?

Some people can take these spontaneous "excursions" via meditation visualization or after a good yoga session. I have also experienced this state during the latter, but frankly, I don't get the same sense of freedom as I do when I take those unexpected and unplanned forays while my body is sleeping. Nevertheless, meditating during the day can be helpful in preparing your body for an astral flight when you sleep. The most important thing in accomplishing an astral flight is to be completely balanced in every aspect of your Being. I have a friend who religiously meditates for one hour every single morning and guess what? She is one of the most balanced individuals I know. Just being around her is soothing and calming. I also might add that she doesn't watch television—ever. If you've just sat and viewed the evening news, forget about being balanced! Astral flying is out! Negativity will predominate. Like a child, you have to have complete trust and self-confidence in the fact that anything is possible. You don't have to force yourself to clear your mind as you attempt to meditate. If it helps you to relax, then certainly use your candles and/or incense and say your mantras. What you need to know, though, is that these preparations are not necessary. If a thought enters your head, go with it, honor the thought, and then dismiss it. As you begin meditation, concentrate on the thought that you are Spirit *first and foremost* and you are temporarily *letting go* of your body while paying a visit to your Higher Self, your Divinity, whatever you believe is the *Real You.* Whatever pops into your mind, don't force yourself to get rid of the thought. Honor it; then dismiss it. You will find that as your meditation begins to take hold, the thoughts that enter will become nonsensical and eventually disappear.

If fear is present in your mind, an astral flight won't happen. The most common fear that people have is that they may not be able to return to their body. Really? Remember that you are already Spirit that is exploring human experiences, so what makes you think that your physicality is ever stronger than your spirituality? In other words, fear of kicking the bucket while astral flying is a waste of energy. You're not going to get rid of your spirit that easily!

People with Eastern religious beliefs have been having out-of-body experiences for centuries, and they don't even need to be asleep while temporarily "escaping" their bodies. A good example of this may be found in the book *Autobiography of a Yogi* by Paramahansa Yogananda. In just one account in his book (among many accounts), Yogananda tells of meeting the spirit of his guru (teacher) and conversing with him, while said guru was actually in a deep meditation a hundred miles away.

Meditating before going to sleep is a good way to relax your fears and doubts as to your spirit's abilities. If this doesn't appeal to you, then just concentrate your thoughts on something pleasant such as a field full of pungent, sweet-smelling flowers or the soothing sounds of a softly flowing stream or a relaxing walk on a beach. Anything that works for you to rid your mind of anxiety and/or fear is fine. Also, it doesn't hurt to ask your Guidance, Higher Self, or Head Honchos (as I refer to my Spirit Guides) to help you to attain that flight of fancy.

Don't expect to accomplish an out-of-body flight immediately when you first try. Practice makes perfect, and patience is the key. The end results of patience and practice are well worth the wait.

There is an ancient Chinese tradition that believes your spirit creates dreams. According to this old belief, Spirit leaves the body while you are dreaming in order to travel to other "worlds" and meet with other Souls. The Master Chuang-tzu (350 BC) is well known to the people of China. He was a writer who appreciated the importance of dreaming and was involved in the development of Taoism, which sees everything as being balanced: yin and yang. The Chinese were exploring metaphysics long before our New Age culture brought it into the forefront of our Western lives, when it became the thing to do among modern-day "discoverers" of other realities.

Most folks are aware of the Chinese method of acupuncture to heal a person suffering from an ailment. Few are aware that for centuries the Chinese have also used dreams to cure physical afflictions. The Chinese had been exploring dreams long before Jung or Freud, and they were studying their dream-time centuries prior to that master of psychics Edgar Cayce introduced the concept to the Western culture. When using dreams to cure illnesses, Chinese practitioners utilize symbols—just as we do to interpret dreams—but primarily they analyze how the person was *feeling* during the dream. Should you wish to delve into their traditions, go for it!

Needless to say the Asians are much more knowledgeable and advanced in this area than their Western counterparts. They accept without question that the spirit, mind, and body cannot be divided. In other words, our life is a Holy Trinity; we are truly Three in One. Our dreams are a reminder of that necessary balance, and they attempt to bring equality between our conscious reality and our spiritual existence. We are also yin and yang.

In similar ways, Native Americans meets their ancestors during their dreams/visions, and their dream-time is considered sacred. The vision quest is also a profound journey to the world of spirit and dreams. Before the Europeans discovered this continent, a lone Native American would go into the wilderness to find guidance and renewal so that his spirit could be revitalized. In preparation for his lonely vigil, this individual would fast and spend days in order to attain that place whereby he could enter the realms of his visions and dreams. Dreams are viewed as a form of the "real world" by the Native American, and they are very much an important facet of their lives.

I've often wondered if this was what Jesus of Nazareth was doing when he spent those solitary, forty days and nights within himself? It's interesting to note that many unexplained mysteries in our world deal with similarities between widely dispersed cultures, such as pyramidal architecture existing in both Egypt and South America. How did two different cultures build the same structures when they were thousands of mile apart in the world? Who built them without communication between these places that are so far away from each other? China and North America are also geographically at the opposite sides of a vast ocean, yet both share similar beliefs regarding dreams. How could people of such different cultures as the Native American and the Chinese have the same dream-time beliefs and ideas? I'm sure that our ancient ancestors didn't rely on computers and cell phones to communicate!

The Indian dreamcatcher originated with the Ojibwa tribe, and although it's become a commercialized product, it's original intent was to protect the slumbering person from having nightmares. Can they also be an aid in escorting one to flights of fancy? Such flights can be very powerful, and it's good to know that in spite of their "cultural modernization" by encroaching settlers, the Native American spiritual traditions are still being honored, followed, and shared.

From time immemorial, cultures from all over the world have followed ancient beliefs about the "Dream-Time." From the lost cultures of South America that existed even before the Incas or Aztecs to the Scandinavian countries of the far northern hemisphere, they all have one commonality. All are aware of the importance of dreams to a Soul's journey. Astral flying—or flights of fancy—are indeed as old as humankind.

Here is one example of a spiritual flight.

Several years ago I was on a retreat with a group of friends. It took place at a lodge situated in one of the dense, magnificent forests that are so abundant in the state of Oregon. We spent five days in quiet contemplation practicing spiritual "homework" and shared with each other our deepest thoughts and feelings. One day we spent twenty-four hours in absolute silence. It was five days of rest and spiritual healing. On our last night there, I had one of the most awesome, lucid/spiritual flights that I've ever had before or since. Although we will talk more in depth about lucid dreaming later, for now I share this experience as a true gift of spiritual flying—combined with lucid mind control. I'll never forget it.

In my dream my spirit flew far out beyond the limits of our earth and was somewhere in the vast, endless Universe. I was viewing an expansive vista of stars, galaxies, and planets that even astronomers haven't discovered. It was absolutely soundless "out there." It reminded me of the Simon and Garfunkel song "Sounds of Silence." Absolute perfection. The sight of such magnificence took my breath away. My Self felt an utter sense of peace beyond what my physicality has never known. The feeling is hard to describe from the narrow limits of a human three-dimensional viewpoint. It's impossible for our spoken words to express the Spirit in all its Wholeness. I suspect that I felt the same peace that people speak of when they've had near-death experiences: indescribable.

Tears began to wet my face as my Soul soaked up this absolute totality of Connection. My thoughts eventually turned to the fact that we humans are such an insignificant dot in this mindless Universe full of mysterious energy-forms. How could we feel so egotistically important when we are as insignificant as a strip of seaweed floating on a mighty ocean?

Then I realized that even though we are only a tiny particle of All That Is, without our presence on this earth plane, the Universe wouldn't be complete. Just as millions of grains of sand are needed to make up a beach, humans are that one grain that is essential to the completion of the Universe. We are essential to the Wholeness of Universal Life. I realized that we are not just an offshoot of Divinity but an indelible *part* of the Divine.

I felt myself returning to my body in the bed and fought the awakening as I didn't want to return from a place of such utter bliss. Of course, I had to. I still had work to do on this earth. Reluctantly I slowly awakened in my bed in that forest-enclosed lodge.

Of course, the preparation for this spiritual journey was intensely relaxing. This retreat is an example of the necessity to be completely *balanced* in physical well-being and spiritual thought. I'm not saying that you have to retreat from the world for a few days, but whatever form takes you to the right sense of communion with Self is a necessity. This experience is an example of flying on a special quest during your sleep. Via your subconscious your flights of fancy have unlimited power, and you can explore anything that you desire. *You are unlimited.* This is one time when my dream-flight experience was a gift that was also a lucid dream. Over time the feeling of utter peace lapsed, but its memory stays with me and still gives me hope for the human race.

Another time when I went astral flying, I was as close to the full moon as an astronaut. It was huge, iridescently glorious, and so empowering! Although this spiritual sojourn was not as impactful as the former dream had been, it was still a journey of solace and renewal. Once again I was in the vastness of outer space and just looking at the moon. What was really breathtaking was that it communicated with me in all its magnificence and knowing. These types of dreams are hard to describe as words are too insignificant for the feeling of *Completeness* they give to the dreamer.

When you are feeling comfortable with your dream-time, you can practice taking yourself on flights of fancy to anyplace you want to go. Just as you can meditate or visualize where you want to be while you're still consciously within the body, you can learn to do the same thing while sleeping. All you have to do before you go to sleep is to *believe that you can.* Keep it simple. Know that you can attain anything you wish because you are Spirit first and foremost. You just happen to be having a human experience.

In order to prepare yourself to experience an astral flight, choose a time/day when you can concentrate on nothing and no one but *you.* An ideal way to accomplish this is, as I have described, by spending at least twenty-four hours in a place of silent retreat, but I know this isn't always feasible. So the next best thing is to make time for yourself to be in a quiet space, even if it's only for ten minutes. Here in the Pacific Northwest I can think of several places that will accommodate me in this area for a short period of time, even my own home surroundings. I live in a semirural area that is encompassed by tall fir trees. Although my neighbors that are on either side of me are only a few yards away from my back garden, I religiously spend time each morning to contemplate the new day. Armed with my first cup of coffee (yes, this is a necessity for me), I sit in a rocker on my porch and, while I rock gently back and forth, listen to the birds, the breeze rustling through the trees, even the distant sounds of traffic rumbling along on our "local" freeway is part of my comfort zone. Then, I quietly go within myself and connect with All That Is. It may be for a brief amount of time, but it's enough to start my day balanced and in tune with my Higher Self. Believe it or not this small ritual stays with me until I go to sleep that evening. I may not have the pleasure of an astral flight, but my dreams are vividly remembered. I'm sure that wherever you live there is a place that is right for you.

If a retreat isn't possible, then find time to be by yourself in your own private space without being interrupted. Naturally, that also means that you must turn off telephones and definitely silence the television. If you live in a large city that has honking horns or sirens blaring outside, make sure that all windows are closed and try to mentally shut out any distracting noise. Then again, if you are used to these noises and they are a familiar part of your environment—like my freeway sounds—they may be a part of your life and therefore unobtrusive. It is not easy to always take time out for yourself, but even in a large city, I'm sure you can find peace and quiet somewhere. My favorite quiet place is an unknown spot at the coast where the only "distractions" are the rumbling of the ocean and the cry of seagulls. Distractions? No way! You may even consider taking a vision quest to get into a spiritual space for dreams and/or visions. There are plenty of facilitators who will gladly show you how to have this experience. Whatever comes forth during a vision quest is still coming from your subconscious or your Higher Consciousness. Anything that is conducive to a balancing of your well-being is an added plus. Yes, balance is the magic word. When you've achieved this state, then just let go and let Spirit take you soaring to any flight that you fancy.

After such a relaxing sojourn, your day is guaranteed to go well. You will be left with a sense of euphoria that will stay with you for hours. After having had such a dream, your mundane routine can take on pleasurable overtones that are very good for you. They are definitely better for you than vitamins or a good massage or even chocolate!

Recap

Astral flying is a state whereby your spirit leaves the body while it's asleep and travels to other worlds. Such experiences are usually remembered as dreams but are in fact a temporary freeing of the spirit from the body.

A similar effect can be experienced via meditation or visualization, but spirit flying is less "controlled" and therefore more satisfying.

You don't have to be an adept at meditation to experience astral flying. But you do have to be balanced and conscious of your spiritual Self. You need to find the time to be in your own "space."

Astral flying is nothing new. It's been around since the beginning of humankind and spans all cultures in various forms. The Chinese have been utilizing astral flying for centuries and believe that they visit with departed Souls during these times. From the Scandinavian countries to the Andes of South America and lush forests of the Amazon, flights of fancy while asleep have been utilized for centuries.

The biggest drawback to an astral flight during sleep is fear of not being able to return to your body. It won't happen. Spirit is more powerful than the body and always returns to complete its human experience.

While you are awake, you can learn to control your mind and practice astral flying in order to experience this phenomenon during your sleep-time. You can prepare your mind for this experience by taking a vision quest, a silent retreat, or going anyplace that is effective for you to obtain balance of body, mind, and spirit; even your own backyard as long as it's quiet.

When preparing to go to sleep, try meditating in whatever form that is comfortable for you and produces the desired effect. If this isn't your cup of tea, just visualize a soothing, quiet place that will relax and clear your mind.

Remember, balance is the magic word.

3

Dreams That Go Bump in the Night

A most intriguing operation of the active subconscious is that people who have passed over are able to visit you in your dreams—literally. All we have to do is be open to welcoming their presence, and they will be there. Trust is the magic word, and of course that old bugaboo named fear is a no-no.

During sleep, when the conscious mind lies dormant, departed loved ones find this time is excellent to enter and talk to you via your dreams. Believe it or not, your subconscious is full of unexplored wonder, and because you have no inhibitions while you're sleeping and less fear, you are more open to receiving "ghosts." Dreams are a very special way in which those who were close to you in life will be able to contact you after they have passed to the "other side." Usually they come to give comfort and solace to loved ones, but many times they also come to prepare you for some occurrence that is about to happen in your life. There are still other times when they simply want to let you know that they are still with you and have come to say "hello."

I have recently reread Moody's famous book from the 1970s titled *Life After Life*. We've come a long way since this doctor's discoveries of life beyond the physical body. However, one passage really resonated with me, as it validated my own belief as to the power of our subconscious minds. Many of his subjects who had had NDEs (near-death experiences) stated that although they were conscious of the fact that they had left their body, they had *clarity of mind* far beyond their previous physicality. Taking this one step further, I suggest that while we are sleeping, our spirit has more unlimited awareness than our puny human consciousness cannot possibly imagine. Personally, from years of "seeing" past lives of clients, I know that when I see an entity's past-life story, and he/she is about to leave the body, that individual is experiencing that same deeper clarity as the person having had an NDE. It's as if the entity's perception has left the limiting "box" of existence on the earth plane. He/she is now seeing far more clearly beyond the outer edges of this planet. The individual simply has more *clarity*. Whenever I have entered into a psychic space whereby I am allowed to see a client's past life, the "death" procedure of the client (during a crossover from physical matter to Spirit) has without exception always been similar to NDEs. The Spirit has an extreme *knowing*, as if it can see beyond the horizon. The entity is conscious of every nuance of the life that he/she has experienced but is now seeing it with more understanding and a clearer vision.

You may be wondering what all this has to do with your dreams and those visitations from departed loved ones? The fact is that when these past-life memories serve a useful purpose to the person's present life, they resurface as dreams with *in-depth clarity*. In this same way, there is more natural expansion and attention to minute details when "dead" people visit you in dreams. This is because the sleeping person is without the limitations of the physical body. The "ghost" will bend over backward to give you validation of its presence and utilize anything to make you certain of the same.

While visiting my husband in the hospital at the end of his life, I entered his room one day just as he was awakening from a deep, pain-releasing, medically induced sleep. As he came out of his sleeping state he said, "I just dreamed that I knew what the world was all about, and it was so simple. But now I've forgotten." To this day I still feel frustrated by those enigmatic words. What did he see while he was asleep? Maybe I'll never know. But as he said, life on this planet would no doubt be simple, if we humans didn't complicate it so much. Most of the time we not only can't see the forest for the trees, we also don't even know that a forest exists!

I have also heard doctors state that when a person dies, the brain continues to operate for several minutes after the heartbeat has ceased. I will take this statement one step further. I believe that this is the time that the dying person has that mindfulness whereby he/she still has one "foot" in the physical world and the other in the world of Spirit. This is when the person is able to see where he/she has come from and whence he/she is returning. It's as if the departing person is viewing the life that is passing via a DVD that is being played on fast-forward. And I believe that dreaming is the closest to the death experience as possible for us while still being in the physical body. Therefore, doesn't it make sense that those who have departed this earth plane find us to be more receptive to their presence when we are in a state of sleep?

At the time of physical "death" the brain is the last to slow down and stop functioning. The body may be dead, but part of your brain isn't and the expansion of the subconscious is never-ending. While sleeping we are as close to their "world" as we ever will be while still retaining a physical life.

Every single event that has ever taken place in our lives from the womb to death is stored in our subconscious. When we are born, we don't just inherit the DNA from our parents, but also at a cellular level we bring back DNA from past-life experiences. And, many of these "DNA cells" remain in your subconscious. When necessary, these experiences will emerge in the form of dreams in order to aid you on your life path. Therefore even people that you may not have known in your present life but have "met" in a previous existence will sometimes visit you in your dreams. This is probably why we sometimes feel the presence of someone but can't pinpoint an actual person. A friend recently shared an experience with me of awakening from sleep and seeing a woman standing near him. She immediately disappeared when he became conscious of her presence, but he was perfectly aware of her image although he didn't know who she was. Our subconscious knows, and sometimes these entities will visit us in our dreams, just for old times' sake. I suggested to my friend that if this happened again, he should try and communicate with the entity. I have experienced dream visits from a maternal grandmother who died long before I was born. Fortunately, I recognize her from family photos that I have.

After the birth of my oldest grandchild, his mother (my daughter) dreamed that her husband's grandmother was leaning over the baby's bassinet talking to him. The dream was so real that she awakened and saw the "ghost," at which point my daughter screamed out in fright. Immediately the grandmother disappeared. I'm sure that most of you have had similar "visits" from people you have known, or maybe not known, in your present life. Fear is a natural reaction if you are not familiar with this phenomena, but it isn't necessary and, if you allow them to communicate with you, they will.

There is a very good book called *Living Images*, written by a woman who was an excellent medium in this life. She's now left this earth, but her book lives on and is the best I have ever read on the subject of departed entities who return to contact their loved ones here on earth. Her name was Coral Polge. I had the pleasure of meeting her on a couple of occasions when I was visiting England and found her to be a very developed and gifted physic. During one visit with her she told me that there was a young woman visiting with me. To make herself known the entity began to tap her chest as if she was having difficulty breathing. Coral was also a gifted artist who was able to draw the images of these visiting spirits. She drew a sketch of a young woman who greatly resembled my oldest sister who had died at the age of eighteen. I barely remember this sister, as I was the "baby" of the family, but I do know that she died of tuberculosis—hence the image of having problems breathing. If you have difficulty in contacting a departed loved one during your sleep-time, the next best thing is to have them contact you through mediumship. I can't emphasize enough that fear is unwarranted. If you receive a visit from a "ghost," you don't have to be too sociable and offer them a cup of tea, but they'd appreciate having you acknowledge their presence with a few words of greeting.

Dreams are a very special way in which loved ones may be able to contact you after they have passed to the "other side." Naturally this can be a great comfort to anyone who is grieving the loss of someone that was close in heart, and whether or not you are aware of their presence, they hang around for as long as you need them, although the average length of time is one year. It's so amazing how much support they can give you during the grieving process.

I have had people tell me of many instances whereby the departed Soul has made itself known to them through their dreams and has even left physical signs for the loved one. Instead of using dream-time as their means of communication, they will sometimes achieve their goal through manifesting incidents that enter the person's everyday life. A recent incident of this nature happened to a friend who had lost his father. While he was driving his mother to the funeral home in order to make the necessary burial arrangements, they came to a traffic light that was red. Naturally they stopped. He noticed that the car stopped in front of them had one of those personalized license plates on the back. The license plate displayed one word only: the name of the friend's deceased father. Coincidence? I choose to believe otherwise.

Another friend was unpacking boxes in her new home. Intermittently she would hear faint, tinkling music and couldn't figure out where it was coming from. She checked various places around the house, but the music seemed to be coming from one of the boxes. Puzzled, she began to unpack the carton and eventually came to the bottom. The only object left was a greeting card. It was one of those newfangled cards that play music when opened. The card was closed and had lain underneath a pile of other stuff in the box, but nevertheless it was playing music. When she opened up the card, she realized it was one that she'd received at an earlier date from a daughter who had been dead for several years. Although this friend is accepting of metaphysical concepts, she is still leery of ghosts. Could this daughter have been trying to contact her via her dreams and, having been "blocked," found this other method of communicating with her mother?

After my husband died, he visited me frequently in my dreams until, after about a year, he stopped. On the last dream/visit that I had with him, he stood at the end of the bed and said, "I have to go now." That was it. When my husband came to say "Goodbye," he was wearing a suit as if he were leaving on a business trip. As his employment on earth required him to do a lot of business traveling, this dream image was not surprising. But what really drew my attention was the tie he was wearing. It was one that I absolutely hated! It was also his favorite among dozens of nice-looking ties, and he consistently wore it for his business trips. The tie was bright red, and I would scathingly refer to it as his "Hemorrhoid Tie"! Of course, he knew I would recognize such a validation. He always did have a sharp sense of humor. Incidentally, I might add that as much as I missed my husband, I didn't miss that tie! This is a good example of how visiting "ghosts" in your dreams make every effort to focus your attention on them in specific ways.

Besides using your sleep-time to contact you, the departed spirit will attempt in every conceivable way to bring to you the necessary comfort you require. They won't leave you until they feel that you can handle your life without their presence

My grandfather was estranged from his daughter (my mother) for most of her adult life. His wife, named Lizzie, had died when my mother was only ten years old. When mother reached the age of eighteen, she introduced grandfather to a woman with whom she worked, someone only eighteen months older than my mother and twenty two years younger than grandfather. He married this girl, who gave him two more children, and she managed to alienate the father from his daughter. As a child, I saw very little of this grandfather, and I'm sure that my mother very much missed her father's companionship. When he was about to pass over, he asked my mother to visit his bedside. He told her that "I dreamed that Lizzie visited me last night. She stood at the end of the bed and talked to me." Grandfather didn't share what Lizzie had said to him, but he asked my mother to forgive him for all the years of his neglect toward her.

There are much more to "ghost" dreams/visions than just a friendly chitchat. Sometimes they visit to make us aware of the error of our ways. Think about the ghost of Marley in Dickens's "A Christmas Carol." That is such a great story and an even greater example of departed entities trying to help those who are straying from the Path of Righteousness.

A more profound example of the lengths a spirit will go to in order to try and contact their loved ones happened, once again, to me personally. It wasn't via a dream, but I'm relating it anyway as it proves how ghosts/spirits are capable of performing miraculous events in order to bring solace to departed loved ones.

I was giving a workshop at a metaphysical store, followed by two days of my giving private past-life readings. Clients usually make appointments well in advance of my attendance for these readings as time/space is limited. The first day, my client (I'll call her Carol) didn't show up for her appointment. This is very unusual, but another person entered the store and spontaneously requested a reading, so regardless, Carol's place was filled. Accident? Of course not! While I attended to this person, the owner of the facility said he would try contacting Carol via the telephone number that she'd left when she'd called to make the appointment. After I had completed my time with the spontaneous person, I approached the owner and asked if he had been able to reach the missing Carol.

He had a look of stupefaction on his face as he declared, "You're never going to believe this." He then proceeded to tell me a strange "ghost" story. Because no one answered the telephone when he called, he had left a message. Moments later, a man called back and said, "You've just left a message on my cell phone, and I haven't a clue what you're talking about! Besides that, I live in Oklahoma." Now, this store is located in Washington, and Oklahoma is halfway across the country from the Pacific Northwest. The store owner explained more thoroughly the reason for the call, and the conversation ended.

A few moments later the man called again. "What did you say that woman's name was?" Reply, "Carol." After a long drawn-out pause the man responded, "That was my wife's name but she died eighteen months ago."

That wasn't the end of this strange event. When we looked at the date that "Carol" had called to make the appointment, *it was two months before my event had been publicly advertised.* And nobody in the store remembered taking the call for the appointment.

The only thing I could surmise was that, because of the man's grief and for reasons unknown to me, Carol had found that the store and my appearance there were a "channel" to use in her attempts to contact her husband.

Possibly this was the only means by which she could find an "opening" to reach him and to let the husband know that she was still with him.

One scenario that I played with was that maybe the husband was closed-minded to the idea that the spirit could still contact the living, in which case, could this have been her way of letting him know that there really is life after life? Regardless, my logic tells me that if departed spirits are able go to such lengths to support those who are left behind, how much easier it must be to talk to them while we are sleeping.

Relatives, friends, and lovers will go to extreme lengths if necessary to contact someone on earth if they feel it's a necessity. Of course, the dreamer must be open to their visit, as even "ghosts" cannot invade a person's free will.

The point to my relating these stories is that Spirit has unlimited capabilities of contacting people on earth, even via modern paraphernalia such as telephones. During sleep, your mind isn't controlled by logical thinking. Your subconscious is in charge. So, doesn't it make sense that those in the world of Spirit can actually talk to you while you are in your slumbers, without having to combat fears or prejudices? The fact is that the world of Spirit must be extremely clever and unlimited in its power to overcome man-made obstacles.

When spirits come to you in your dreams, it is usually to remind you that they are still close to you and probably more so in "death" than they were in life. By the same token, they are free to guide you whenever needed, as their "vision" is no longer limited to a physical body. This is why they visit you in your dreams. And, when all else fails, they manifest through physical means, as I'm sure was the case with the woman who needed to contact her husband living in Oklahoma. They may also become a Spirit Guide, if you will.

One more book that I strongly recommend is *A Man Called Peter*—written by his wife, Cathleen Marshall. Peter Marshall was an Episcopalian minister, who during the 1940s became the chaplain for the United States Congress. Although his faith was that of a "standard vanilla" Christian church, his life was far from standard. His God was his best friend with whom he had long conversations as one would have with any best friend. His wife was devastated by his untimely death and grieved profoundly.

One night she had a dream that she saw him tending roses in Heaven's garden. In life, Peter had loved his garden and spent as much time as possible taking care of his roses. In the dream he told his wife that he now had as much time as he wished to take care of the roses and was thoroughly enjoying himself. No symbols to decipher. This was just a straightforward dream message of support and comfort for the grieving wife.

Apart from this incident that validates visits of the departed via dreams, the book is full of metaphysical events that happened in his life and is an awesome read. *A Man Called Peter* is a testament to one man's faith and trust in a Divine Being. If you are not a bookworm, then you may want to rent the movie that was made from Peter Marshall's life story. It was produced during the 1950s and nominated for several Academy Awards.

∾

My grandson recently shared with me a dream that he had of an uncle (his father's youngest brother) who died tragically in a car accident at the age of eighteen. At the time of the uncle's death my grandson was a very small boy and his "Uncle Ken" had taken him under his wing. He had built a good relationship with the little boy.

During this particular dream that he'd had, Uncle Ken had visited him, and my grandson called me to get my input. Because of the dream's scenario, I was convinced that this uncle was trying to bring a message to my grandson. So I told him that when he went to bed that night, he needed to ask for a revisit from his uncle, so that he could *listen* to what he was trying to tell him.

I should like to reiterate that when talking to the "dead," you must give them permission to come into your will in order for them to talk to you. This is a must. Your willpower is there for a reason, and no one may invade it unless you give permission—not even "ghosts."

Unbeknownst to my grandson, his grandfather (the uncle's father) was seriously ill. Before he had time to call on the spirit of his uncle again, he received a phone call to let him know of his grandfather's death. Of course, his uncle had been trying to prepare him for this and was using the dream-world to contact him.

Now the most significant aspect of my grandson's dream was an incident that happened afterward. Uncle Ken validated his visit by leaving tangible proof. Apparently after this dream, my grandson was beginning to awaken and felt cold. He had only a sheet covering his body but a folded blanket lay at the foot of the bed. As he was coming out of the dream-state, he was thinking that he needed to pull the blanket up from the bottom of the bed, but before he could do so, he found that the blanket was already around his shoulders. Did he dream that only a sheet covered his body, or was Uncle Ken protecting his "little nephew"? Regardless, I'm convinced that Uncle Ken was using the dream-state to communicate with my grandson and was still taking care of him.

I could go into long detail explaining all the clinical and psychological reasoning regarding dreams, but of course, I'm a "show me" person. I need tangible proof of any subject. That is why I am giving you personal, tangible proof of the power of the Spirit world in linking to you through your dreams. I also could spend hours sharing more proof I've received over the years, but just one more example of the ingenuity of departed spirits and I'm done!

When I first came to the United States, I was engaged to a young man from New York. We had met while he was serving as a GI in Britain, and after a whirlwind romance he'd asked me to marry him. It was one of those connections that usually only happen once in a lifetime when two young people meet and instantly fall in love. Without going into all the specific reasons as to why we didn't marry, I'll just say the engagement was broken off, and we eventually lost touch with each other.

Fifty years later and by "accident" (ah-ha) we came into contact again—via the Internet, no less. He was married to a lovely lady (we've since become friends), but he was very ill and died soon after this reconnection. Shortly thereafter I had the opportunity to visit New York, and his widow asked me to spend a few hours with her at her home before leaving.

I was due to leave for New York on a Monday, and the previous day (Sunday) I attended a service at my favorite Spiritualist church. I have to say that the mediums that lead this church are very spiritually minded and extremely gifted. And if you have difficulty communicating with "ghosts" via your dreams, a visitation with a good medium is the next best thing. After the service, the medium who was holding the service that day approached me and said, "May I come to you, Marie?" At the risk of repeating myself, I remind you that no one can "invade your space" without permission, and good mediums never forget this fact. After I gave her the okay, she proceeded to tell me that there was the spirit of a young man standing by my chair. "He wants me to say to you, 'May I have this dance?'" Immediately I felt cold chills go through my body and knew to whom she was referring. The young man and I had first met at a local dance hall in England, where he'd approached me and spoken those very same words.

After the service the medium accurately described the young man's physical appearance and said, "He was standing by your chair all through the service."

But even more profound was the dream I had just after this incident. Without going into personal detail, this dream was a message of why it wasn't necessary for us to marry in this life. The dream was extremely helpful to me in reconciling my guilt at having broken off the engagement all those years past. I *listened* and my guilt was gone.

~

Yes, "ghosts" do visit your dreams while you are sleeping or anytime that your mind is open to receiving them. But those are the magic words. *You need to be open to their visit.* And, it goes without saying that they can bring great comfort to those they've left behind. Their contact is a gentle nudge that they give to remind you that there is no such thing as death. You don't have to learn any special ritual. There's no need to meditate. Light incense and candles if you so desire, but they aren't a necessity either. It's very simple. Get rid of your fear and inhibitions. Enjoy a personal visitation through your dreams.

Recap

Dreams of "ghosts" are usually visitations by people that were close to us in life and are now visiting to bring comfort to the grieving loved one. They usually stay around for approximately one year until they feel you have recovered from your loss.

Sometimes, you may dream of being visited by someone you don't know. It could be someone who was with you in a prior life and is now a spirit guide. All you have to do is ask questions. You'll get the answer.

Whenever a spirit visits you in a dream, you must give that spirit permission to talk with you. Nothing or nobody may invade your free will.

Spirit/ghosts will visit to warn you of some event that is about to take place in your life, comfort you in your grief, or just to say "hello" to you.

Should you feel qualms at having a visitation while sleeping, a good medium or Spiritualist church is always another path to explore in order to contact departed Souls.

If a spirit has difficulty in getting through to you, that spirit will usually find other means by which to make contact. There is no limit to Spirit's abilities.

You don't have to have any particular religious beliefs to access spirits/ghosts, as proven via the story of Peter Marshall's life, among others.

If you are having difficulty in recognizing the visiting entity, know that spirits will go out of their way to give you a sign that will light up your memory and validate the appearance.

Last but not least, eliminate any fear you may have. Don't be reticent in the face of "ghosts" in your dreams. An open mind is definitely needed.

"Seek and you will find. Listen and the door will be opened for you."

∽ 4 ∾

Past-Life Dreams

Whether you believe in reincarnation or not, it doesn't make any difference when it comes to dreaming. Your subconscious doesn't think, "Oh! Forget this person! He/she doesn't believe they've lived previous lives, so it's no use having someone from their past to attempt to contact them." Sounds ridiculous, doesn't it? Your subconscious doesn't rationalize. It is a part of your physicality and, like the rest of your brain, operates as automatically as when it tells you that you need to visit the bathroom! You have to remember that it's that part of your brain that is your "bank vault." Remember, your subconscious stores everything you have placed there, whether you're aware of this or not. Therefore dreams give you the opportunity to work out karma from your past that you may be having difficulty in consciously taking care of in your present existence.

Indulge me for a moment and play a game with me. Imagine, if you will, that you're getting ready to be born. You have made a "contract" between yourself and the Divine that when you get to earth you will accomplish certain tasks. You might be thinking to yourself, "When I get to earth, I'll do such and such a thing, and this, and that, and I'll work on perfecting my spiritual growth. It's going to be a breeze!" Wham! You are born and guess what? You've forgotten what it was that you came to do. What a bummer! Not to worry—your subconscious remembers. And whenever necessary, it will remind you through your dreams. Just keep in mind that you are still Spirit having a human experience and can tap into your real Self anytime you wish.

Dreams that channel a previous incarnation usually surface when something in your past is still affecting your life in the present. It might be a physical ailment that you still carry or an emotional scar that still haunts you. You may be experiencing feelings of guilt—but you don't understand why—or fears that seem to have come from no logical place. At the opposite end of the spectrum, there could be a gift that you've brought with you that you had developed in another life. I'm convinced that Mozart didn't compose music at such a tender age without having practiced his art during another lifetime. Could Einstein really have developed such genius during the limited expanse of his one lifetime?

The following is an example of someone who needed to know why she was having difficulties in her life and how a past-life dream gave her the answer. I'll call her Joan.

Joan came to me to have a past-life reading. We were taken back in North American history to the time of "white man's" first landing on the shores of the East Coast. In that life Joan had been a squaw. This squaw was extremely spiritual and like most of the native Indians, greatly honored Mother Earth. She unquestioningly lived the spiritual life of her ancestors. Her people welcomed the "palefaces" with open arms and loving naivety. But Joan in her past life was also a seer, and through her* visions/dreams was saddened by what she saw to be the future for her people. She felt helpless in the face of the events that she foresaw in her visions; that is, the white man's betrayal of her people. Feeling herself unable to stop the harsh treatment inflicted on her kinsmen, she was saddened and frustrated at the loss of the Indians' native way of life. Because of the times that she lived in and the rules of her people, whereby the female was taught to be submissive and keep her mouth shut (Gloria Steinem would have had a field day in those times) the squaw thought, "I am only a woman and, as such, unable to stop the white man's plundering." She saw the future and knew that the land and her people's Sacred Space would be violated.

After the reading ended, Joan shared a dream with me that she'd had that seemed to connect with this past life. "I was in the backseat of my car," she said "and my husband was driving. As we traveled along the highway, I saw animals coming toward us, racing along each side of the car. On one side were animals led by a cougar. On the other side were a herd of white buffalo."

Awesome! Joan's subconscious was jogging her past-life memories as the Indian seer in order to show her something about her personality. She needed to have awareness of her continued submissiveness. She needed to remember *who she really is* and her purpose here in this lifetime. The cougar represented not only her totem but her present life. The cougar (or mountain lion) is one of the swiftest animals that there is, but even though it can run exceedingly fast, it tires easily due to the amount of speed it uses. In

---

* *During these times in American history, the term "Native American" was unknown. The titles used were "Indian" and "Squaw" for a female. Likewise the European settlers were know by the native Americans as "White Man" or "Pale Faces."*

her present life she was trying to give to others too much of herself and exhausting her energies—just as the Indian woman had given wholeheartedly to the palefaces. She was "running so fast" she was depleting her energy.

She was sitting in the backseat of her car. Taking a backseat in her life. "I am only a woman."

A car in a dream is your transportation through life. It's your physical body and whatever is happening with that car is happening to you. Joan was "taking a backseat" in her present life and continuing to dishonor the woman that she really is. Instead of thinking of herself as "only a helpless woman," she needed to be reminded that she had returned with the sensitive, but strong female power from that previous life. She no longer had to be submissive, the difference being that she now lives in an age where women are respected for their knowledge and intelligence. And furthermore she is living in an age when Native Americans are reclaiming their place in this land. It's time for the interlopers to pay their karmic debts. But Joan was still in that submissive mode. She was allowing her "husband" (dominant figure) to do the driving because she thought of herself as "just a woman" and not equal to a man's strength. She was still acting the part of the helpless Indian maiden who was used to being submissive to the Indian male warrior.

The "husband" in control of her car was that aspect of *herself* that was supposed to be in control. Usually (but not always, depending on the situation) other people in our dreams are reflections of ourselves. In this scenario the "husband" driving the car was that aspect of Joan (male, warrior self) that needed to get back into the driver's seat. *She was giving her power away instead of empowering herself.* By the same token, maybe she was literally allowing her husband to tell her what to do! The amazing thing about dreams is that the same dream may be giving a literal message as well as a metaphorical one. It covers all aspects of one's life.

The white buffalo is such a profound symbol in Native American lore. It was said that when a white buffalo was born there would come a time of peace for the Indians. The Native American Nation would once more return to their own power. A few years ago a white buffalo was born to a ranch in the upper Midwest and people flocked from all over the country to acknowledge this event. Joan's dream had shown her a complete herd of white buffalo. Wow! What goes around comes around. Honor and peace would return for the Indians—and also for this Indian seer.

This past-life dream was reminding Joan of who she really is. She is no longer helpless to do anything about outside forces that were creating problems in her life. Just as we all do, Joan was creating her own reality and needed to change her submissive self and honor her own self-esteem. She needed to recognize that loving, nurturing, and strong female who is still a part of her Soul. It was time for her to take back control of her life.

Joan needed this validation from her past life as to why she had returned to this present time. She needed to honor the "contract" she had made with herself and the Divine and not "take a backseat" to her power. She no longer needed to feel subservient. She was given this dream from her past to help her journey in the present.

At a much later date, Joan was bringing her mother to my home to have a reading, and via an incident that seemed to have been preordained, she was given the opportunity to apply her seer's abilities. Although at this time she didn't realize it, she was still a seer as the following account will verify.

I have a pet cat that I *don't* own; she owns me. I'm sure pet owners can relate to this situation. Because I live in an area where wild animals such as coyotes and raccoons roam at night, I keep my pet in the house at all times. Consequently, whenever she finds an opportunity to escape to the great outside world, she does. On the day that Joan was visiting, she sneaked outside when I carelessly left a door ajar. I didn't miss her for a few hours, but when I did, I immediately went into panic mode. After what seemed like an eternity of searching the neighborhood and knocking on doors to enquire if anyone had seen a black furry escape artist, I finally gave up and returned home.

As I waited for my company in a stressful state, the most horrible scenarios as to what my cat's fate might be flashed though my mind. What if by nightfall I still hadn't found her? I envisioned some ravenous coyote enjoying a tasty, cat meat appetizer! By the time Joan and her mother arrived I was far from serene! Needless to say I certainly was not in the right frame of mind to give a reading for Joan's mother.

They were both understanding, and after sharing a pot of tea to calm down and visiting for a while, Joan suddenly made a suggestion. "Why don't you leave your back door open? I feel as if she'll find her way back that way." Naturally I was open to any helpful ideas, so did as she suggested. Surprise, surprise! As I opened the back door, there sat my cat waiting patiently to be let in!

It goes without saying that I felt very foolish. What made me think that a cat couldn't find its own way home? I must have been out of my mind! She wasn't so dumb as to stay outdoors permanently. Why? Because there was always plenty of cat food in her dish without her having to hunt mice for sustenance. Even more important, instead of having to roam the nighttime hours and risk having to fight off "enemies," she had a warm bed to sleep in (mine), which she kindly allows me to share.

But how did Joan know my cat was outside the door? Via her seer's ESP of course. Naturally she was delighted that she'd known where my cat was even though she'd never thought of herself as having such gifts. The point is that Joan was unconsciously validating for herself the natural gifts that she had. This incident was an opportunity for her to once more use them. At a subconscious level Joan still retains the gifts that she used in her life as the Indian woman.

Everyone, even you dear reader, has abilities that they may not use, because they can't believe that they have such gifts. But if you believe that you have untapped "jewels" in your personal "treasure chest," all you have to do is open the lid. If you are having difficulty in finding the right key to disclose the contents of your wealth, then what do you do? *Ask for help in your dreams.*

Humanity is receiving numerous worldwide signals that we are at the end of an era in our life on this planet and in the midst of major changes. Apart from all the natural disasters that the media so quickly reports, there are thousands of exciting events that are happening to the "average Joe," people like Joan who are returning to empower themselves. I have experienced hundred of clients' dreams that are their past-life experiences, and they have validated why they have returned at this chaotic point in the timeline of our history. For the most part, they are "old Souls" and, like Joan, are being reminded through their dreams as to why they decided to return now.

Just as Joan was being told of her purpose through a past-life dream, so can you if you're willing to listen. When you feel that there is something more that you're supposed to be doing with your life, ask for answers through your dreams. If what you're experiencing in your present life originated in a past life, it will come forth if you are willing to allow it to and take heed of its message. If you don't understand what the dream is trying to tell you, ask for another dream that will clarify it for you. Your subconscious will be happy to oblige in whatever form is necessary for your understanding and spiritual growth.

There's nothing magical in receiving messages from your past in your dreams. All you have to do is *believe*. If you are having a problem that is making you feel like you've come up against a blank wall, it may be a lesson from your past that is unresolved. Don't be afraid to ask for help from your dreams. Or, if you've never considered the idea that the problem may have come from a past life, be open to this possibility and, again, ask for answers. Past-life dreams are usually a gentle nudge that show you the commitment you made before you incarnated. Also, as in Joan's case, they make you aware of the weaknesses and strengths from the past that you have carried with you into this life, so that you may have the opportunity to do what you're supposed to be doing. We are never given more than we can bite off and chew. Our personalities are made up of pluses and minuses in equal measure. It's up to us to decide which ones we use. Your dreams are one of the pluses that we automatically all have. It's up to you whether or not you want to make the most of them. There's no hard work involved. All you have to do is to be open-minded and respect the messages that dreams bring to you.

I have a chronic problem with neck pain due to damage incurred during an incident with a tornado that I will tell you about later. Unfortunately I drove into it. This neck injury has gradually become worse as the years have advanced. Twice I have had past-life dreams that showed me why I've carried this problem from lifetime to lifetime.

In an ancient Roman life I was killed by a spear (caused by my own folly) that struck the back of my neck and consequently brought about my death. In another past-life dream I lived and died during a medieval European incarnation as a result of being tortured on the rack. My body was wrenched apart. Obviously I'm a slow learner! Even though my subconscious has stored these memories and reminded me of them via dreams of my past existences, I still carry the physical scars with me. Although I realize what I need to do, I'm still learning the lesson. My excuse for still carrying the neck pain is that it reminds me not to repeat that former underlying personality weakness. I try not to be a "pain in the neck" anymore. Yet I still have a tendency to "stretch" myself to the limits of endurance. When this happens, I think on that medieval life, slow down, and get a good body massage, or if that isn't feasible, sit still and relax with a good book.

Edgar Cayce advocated keeping a notebook and pen by your bedside, so that immediately after you awaken you can write down your dream before it escapes your conscious mind. I strongly advise those people who say they don't dream (or have difficulty recalling their dreams) to follow this advice. Within minutes of awakening you will forget a lot of the details of a dream, and by recording it as soon as possible you're more likely to remember its significant bits. If you are convinced that you don't dream, ask to remember. It's that simple. It's also more important for you to write what you do remember as soon as you awaken as within minutes of awakening you will be more likely to forget details of the dream.

I have to confess that I personally don't follow this sound advice, as from years of practice my dreams usually remain clear to me. This is just as well since I can barely open my eyes in a morning, never mind start writing! I don't function without first having a cup of coffee. However, I've learned that people who have studied their dreams from childhood are usually adept at remembering them without the aid of the written word. This may happen to you if you're one of these people. But, if you are new to dream study and especially if you have difficulty remembering their details, I strongly urge you to follow Cayce's suggestion.

It is also a good idea to keep a dream journal and record your dreams on a daily basis. This is a practice that I do follow. By making this a routine you will find that over time, your dreams will read like an ongoing story. Give your dream a title when journaling. Place the date at the top of the page. It's also important to record your *feelings* during the dream. If you have a sense of a certain smell while experiencing the dream-story, write it down. I have found that when I look back over dreams, they seem to follow a pattern, depending on what I'm being guided to do. They have shown me that when I've followed their direction my life has taken a smoother path. By the same token I can see those instances when I've not followed their advice, especially a warning dream, and consequently life has been more difficult.

If a dream is from the "past," it isn't necessary to know that whole life story. The dream will show you what you need to apply to your present situation. Example: if in the dream scenario you are feeling anger, it will show you why. The same applies to any emotion that involves an unresolved issue.

Don't brush off a dream that may seem strange and out of place to you, especially if it is repetitive. More than likely it's a dream from your past trying to help you with your life now. Here again is a very prime example.

As a young girl I sometimes had the same dream with a different scenario but the same feelings and time period. In the dream I was living in the Victorian era and saw myself as a "Crinoline Lady." In other words, I was a woman dressed in the full-skirted attire of the 1800s. I wore a "poky bonnet" that tied underneath my chin with large satin ribbons. The dreams varied in story line and seemed insignificant, but the *feeling* was always the same. There was always a familiar sense of loneliness and extreme sadness.

After becoming an adult and no longer having the dream, I forgot about it, that is, until about twenty-odd years ago. I was hypnotized and taken back in time to a past life I had led in 19th-century England. (Obviously, I gravitate to this country.) I saw myself in that life as the Victorian woman of my dreams. Under circumstances which I thought were beyond my control (we do have the free will to choose our life paths), I created a life for myself that was indeed sad and lonely. I call it my "Wasted Life." It was full of "what might have been" and "should have done," and it was indeed a lonely existence. The story that emerged while under hypnosis told me the reason why I continued to have this repetitive dream, and when I was ready to rectify those mistakes, I was given the past-life dream that showed me what *not* to do again. Once I had "made amends" to myself, I never had the dream again. Having seen that life of waste has made me appreciate the fact that whatever efforts I put into my life's journey are likewise returned a hundredfold in bounty. Each day I remind myself that the past is no more, and the future is unknown. I live for today in mindfulness.

If you have a chronic physical ailment that cannot be cured by medical science, it may stem from a previous lifetime. If you suspect this to be the case, ask to be given a dream that will enlighten you as to why you still carry the ailment. Naturally, it's not enough to know why. You also need to correct the underlying cause. If it's an emotional issue that is causing the physical problem, the dream will usually guide you toward the "cure." The nice thing about your subconscious is that it won't leave you stranded or facing a brick wall. The dream will show you the right direction to take so that you may remove the dead-end situation.

If it's an emotional and/or a mental issue that makes you feel as if you're tangled in a web of no escape, same action applies. Sometimes it's hard to disentangle yourself, especially if it's a problem with a relationship. But if you *really* want to get out of the web, you can! The dream will not only tell you why you're stuck in a quagmire but also show you what you need to do to get to firm ground. However, just like that saying "You can lead a horse to water but you can't make him drink," it's your decision as to whether you want to "quench your thirst" and get rejuvenated or continue to be led to the trough (dream) and balk!

Recap

A past-life dream is usually your subconscious giving you a clue as to what you have committed to accomplish or resolve in this lifetime. It makes no difference whether or not you believe in reincarnation. Your subconscious doesn't care!

A past-life dream is usually an unresolved issue that needs your attention in order to move forward with your life's experiences. Like a boomerang, a situation will continue to return to you until you have learned the lesson.

Dreams may bring forth a gamut of human emotions, and this is especially true with past-life scenarios. Deep-rooted feelings of fear or guilt or low self-esteem are not easy to resolve unless you know the cause. Past-life dreams are like a professional counselor who digs deeply to get to the root of the problem.

Common symbols in dreams may be easily interpreted according to the scenario of the dream, but it is advisable to create your own symbols that pertain to you and only you.

If a dream seems to be strange and at the same time also familiar to you, it may be a dream from your "past." Past-life dreams are usually a reminder as to why you have returned again and what "path" you need to be following.

If a dream from your past repeats more than once, you need to pay attention. There is obviously something important that you need to be aware of.

If you don't understand the dream, ask to have it clarified via another dream.

Keeping a dream journal is a good idea for any dreamer but even more so if it's a past-life dream because it's usually a reminder of something you've "contracted" to do in this lifetime.

If you are suffering from a physical, emotional, or mental ailment and you cannot find a "cure," ask to see if it's a past-life trauma that you've returned to resolve. It's no good taking an aspirin to cure a headache if the underlying cause of the head pain is unknown. Usually past-life dreams are telling you the cause.

⌐ 5 ⌐

Asking Your Dreams for Help

I've already covered individual cases when you can ask your dreams for help, such as past lives coming forth in dreams, but as people have a tendency to push this to their back burner, I'll cover it more thoroughly here. Why do some people—even those who firmly believe in their dream messages—tend not to ask for help from their dreams? It's simply hard for some humans to accept as fact that there is an unseen world beyond our three-dimensional physical environment that is in continuous operation. Logic tells some folks that if we can't see it, then it doesn't exist; it must be our imagination.

Recently I encountered a situation that really hit me full blast as to how little people trust the unseen; some even fear the unknown. A woman who is a friend of one of my children left a frantic message on my voice mail. She desperately needed to talk to me. When I called back, she was very upset because her mother was dying. Some members of her family lived in other states and were planning to visit the mother in June. It was March when the mother learned of these plans, and she told her daughter, "Tell them it'll be too late. I won't be here."

While she was relaying this conversation to me, I could tell by the break in her voice that she was on the verge of tears. She didn't want to face the fact that her mother was leaving, which is understandable as none of us enjoy the passing of a loved one. Then the woman told me of the real reason why she had called me. "My daughter was taking a bath, and all at once a spirit appeared to her wearing black and told her that her grandmother was leaving very soon." The woman told me that both she and the daughter were very upset by this visitation, and she asked me, "What does this mean?"

I was taken aback by her question. What could be more obvious than the fact that Spirit was telling her, in plain English, the truth? The spirit world was attempting to prepare the family for the mother/grandmother's departure. No doubt because of their emotional upheaval, their guides were trying to ease their burden. But their grief and consequent horror were keeping them in denial.

I had to gather my wits and answer the woman with sensitivity. I realized that what was obvious to me wasn't so obvious to her and her daughter. The first emotion we feel when a loved one is dying is denial. Yet the girl had been privy to such a clear visitation with a very literal message, and she and her mother were too fearful and emotionally bereft to believe it. This was an "unreal" presence in their logical thinking and *not* a physical person, such as a doctor, who would tell them the truth. Naturally I realized the woman's state of mind and, as gently as I could, validated for her and her daughter the spirit's declaration. Added to this woman's fright was the fact that the spirit was wearing *black*. Ominous, right? Wrong. Here again I had to explain that black was a symbol of change, and even though it could in our minds symbolize the Grim Reaper, for the dying parent/grandparent, the change was going to be for the better. She would no longer be in pain, and she was ready to leave. A few days later I ran into the woman in a supermarket, and thankfully she was much calmer. She told me that her mother had died shortly after the daughter had received the message. It was a relief to see that this woman had recovered her equilibrium and was no longer in denial and afraid.

This was a good reminder for me as to how the fear of death and the unseen world can keep many people from accepting Spirit's help.

While you are sleeping, your conscious mind is resting, breathing is shallow, and your body is in repose. You are now in that never-never land between life and death. This is when your subconscious brain activates and starts to work without being hampered by your everyday activities and busy thoughts. This is when you are free of physical encumbrances, so that you may safely ask for help with any problem you are having. You can guarantee that your subconscious is getting the message and going to bat for you on the issue. It works on the "night shift" in a way that is remarkably efficient. The dreams that your subconscious brings forth at this time can literally be telling it to you "like it is" as well as metaphorically conveying a subtler message to you. Whatever the dream is telling you, it's designed to help in solving your problem.

To own your personal power while dreaming, you have to believe wholeheartedly that you can. Visualize yourself diving to the depths of an ocean to see what long-lost treasures you can find. You discover a perfect treasure chest that's lain at the bottom of the sea for centuries. Although it is covered in algae and rusty with age, you're still able to raise the lid and look inside. Behold! You see solid gold bullion, rare flashing gems that blind your eyes with their brilliance, wonderful and mysterious objects that leave you feeling breathless! That treasure chest is your subconscious mind. Those priceless artifacts are all the experiences that you've ever had, good or bad—because there is no such thing as "bad" or "good" in the universal consciousness. There are only experiences. These treasures are yours. All you have to do is dive in and take ownership. It's that simple. Asking for help is your right.

As you settle down for a good night's sleep, ask to remember your dreams. Does this sound hokey? It's not. "Ask and it will be given to you; seek, and you will find." Forget the mantras, the rituals, the candles, the incense, and just ask your Higher Self, your angels, archangels, Spirit Guides, God, in whatever form you envision the Divine, to help you remember. You are asking to open your own "treasure chest."

If you feel as if you're trying too hard, just stop! Contacting your subconscious in order to ask for assistance is like searching for the right station on the radio. If you are fiddling with the radio's buttons and continually receiving nothing but static or, even worse, some type of blaring music that you abhor, stop trying so hard! Relax. Slow down and "tune in to your radio station" with mindfulness.

Why do we humans have to make life so difficult? It's because of the times we live in. Most days our bodies are rushing hither and thither while our minds are on the fast track. We live like a roadrunner going a hundred miles an hour. Beep Beep! Brrrr Brrr! Slow down! Turn your cell phone off; ignore that computer or TV;

take a deep breath. Whoever is texting you, the message will still be there tomorrow. Facebook or whatever other social media you use isn't going to go away overnight, and you can guarantee that the TV will continue to broadcast the latest catastrophe whether you are watching or not. Relax and let your subconscious take over. Even better, prepare yourself to have your problem taken care of while sleeping. Sit down and tune in to your Inner Self. Be in this moment. That's the time to ask for help with problem solving. Sometimes you will get your answer while in this state, but if not, when you do drop off to sleep, your subconscious can go to work without hindrance from you Consciousness. You've already prepared your mind and body, now Spirit can take over.

To prove my point, I'll tell you a personal story. Yes, another one. Several years ago my children chipped in and purchased a Mother's Day ring for me. I really treasure that ring and only wear it on special occasions. When it isn't on my finger, it's hanging on a key chain hook attached to a wall by my front entrance.

One day I planned on wearing it to an event and went to retrieve it from its resting place. The ring wasn't there. Not to worry, for whatever reason I'd probably placed it in my jewelry box. I looked, and no, it wasn't there either. Now, I knew that I hadn't removed the ring while outside the house, as this I would never do.

After a month of emptying every drawer and tearing the house apart, looking under couch cushions, moving furniture, etc., the ring still was nowhere to be found. I even took the covers off the air vents to see if it had fallen into one of them. On the positive side, my house was cleaner than it has ever been. But alas, the ring had disappeared. Naturally, being a devout coward, I didn't dare tell my kids what had happened. So, in desperation as I prepared to go to sleep one night, I begged my "Head Honchos" to give me a dream that would tell me where the ring was hiding. "Hey! I hope you're listening because I desperately need help. While I'm asleep *ple-e-ease*, pretty please tell me where the ring is hiding!" You can ask in whatever way is comfortable for you. My guides are used to my habit of getting down to the nitty-gritty without preamble when I need their assistance, and they don't seem to mind. In other words, *I let go and let God.*

Now, I don't remember the story line of my dream as I went into a really deep sleep, but I do remember that the ring was featured in it. Awakening in the morning, I sat up in bed and stared at my open bathroom door. As always, there were two or three robes hanging on a hook on the door, including one I rarely wear. Without any hesitation I got out of the bed, walked over to this particular robe, and felt in a pocket. There was my ring. Of course, I then remembered how it had landed there! I'd returned home one night and, being very tired, took off my clothes and slipped into the robe while preparing to take a shower. Realizing that I still had the ring on a finger, I took it off and slipped it into a pocket. Of course, I intended to hang it back on the key ring hook after I'd showered. And of course, I just forgot.

The point is that this is an example of how your subconscious mind will work for you while you are sleeping. All you have to do is to simply ask for help, get out of the way of yourself, and let your dreams take over. If what you are asking for is in your own best interests, you'll be given the answer when it's the right time for you.

This following dream-story came to me via a client, and I'm sharing it because its message is a reminder to all of us that, in spite of our efforts to upset the natural order of things, the Divine Force never deviates from Unconditional Love. It's a dream that will help anyone who is trying to make sense of the insane events that take place in our everyday world.

This client contacted me and asked my help in interpreting a dream she'd had. The request came shortly after that diabolical shooting spree at the school in Newtown, Connecticut. Unless you've been living in isolation, I'm sure you're very much aware of this tragedy. Its shock waves affected the whole of this continent and beyond.

This highly sensitive and spiritual person shared with me that this seemingly mad act that killed innocent children had affected her so deeply, she couldn't get it from her mind. She felt a sense of despair that wouldn't leave. So one night when she retired to her bed, she prayed that she would get answers that would help her to make sense of it and hopefully regain her personal balance. This dream was such a profound message for her and validation for anyone that needs to be reminded of who we are and where we came from. It's a reminder of our own Divine Oneness of Soul.

The following is this dream, verbatim:

> I was sitting on a white sandy beach on a white wooden bench. On the bench a few feet away from me sat a young man of around eighteen. He was with his family, Mother, Father, three brothers. He had two brothers that were quite a bit younger than him and one brother that was around sixteen years of age. His brothers were playing with the parents on the beach near

the water. The Mother was holding one of the younger boys and kissing him on the neck making him laugh very loudly while the two of them spun around and around. It made me laugh to watch them. The Father was white and the mother was dark skinned. The younger brothers were of mixed races. The two older brothers were white.

The young man who sat on the bench near to me started a conversation. In the conversation I asked him if that was his family, and he said yes. We talked about his younger brothers, and he told me he was concerned because his younger brothers were not family oriented. I told him not to worry because they were still very young and as they grew and matured they would have more love of family. He smiled at that and said he hoped that would happen. Then he got up from the bench and went to where his family was. They began picking up their belongings and getting ready to leave. I really didn't want them to leave, and I closed my eyes hoping that when I opened them they would be gone and I would not have to watch them leave. I sat with my eyes closed for awhile, and when I opened my eyes one of the younger brothers was standing right next to me. This little boy held his hand out to me. I held his hand, and as I did he bowed deeply to me. I looked over to see his family standing about twenty feet from me. When I looked at them they were standing in a line, and they all bowed to me. When I saw them do this I stood up and bowed back to them.

This dream shows how Spirit bends over backward to help individuals when we ask and as I've said, it's also a validation for all people who are concerned about the seemingly spiritless times we live in. The following is my answer/interpretation to the recipient of this awesome dream.

There are so many messages within this dream, but all come down to one simple answer: Unconditional Love. In our world these two words are bandied around so loosely, but few realize their true meaning.

Before I begin to go into the details of this dream, I'll share with you my own beliefs as to the loss of those very special, young lives in Newtown. Over the past twenty-odd years I've been "seeing" varied past lives for people who have come to me for answers about their existence here on earth. But, until a few years past, I never gave a reading for a child. My reasoning was that I felt that such young people were too close to their "home" to need my assistance, and their young intellects wouldn't understand the meaning of reincarnation. Then, over a short period of time several mothers approached me asking to have a reading for their child, and so I felt that for whatever reason I was being led to honor their requests.

Over a period of about two years, I saw approximately six children, ranging from twelve to fifteen. When I was led through the first child's "past," I was awestruck at what I saw, and my emotions were deeply touched. Then with each succeeding child that came to me I experienced the same sense that I was in the presence of a wondrous spiritual being. These children were extremely old Souls. They did not need to be here as their spirits had progressed far beyond anyone else here on earth. It was humbling for me to bear witness to why these children were here. It is hard to describe their spirits from a human perspective, as our meager vocabulary is too limited. All I can say is that these old Souls were the strongest and Godliest I have encountered. And, most important, they were not here to fulfill any karmic debt. They have *volunteered* to come to earth to help humanity clean up the mess we have made of our lives and this planet. They love this planet and its inhabitants so much they are willing to perform any task to save our lives, even as far as forfeiting their own lives when necessary. Seeing the lives of these few children was the biggest gift I have ever received. Among the many gifts that clients have given to me by allowing me to enter their psyche, these children were the Hope Diamond amidst many priceless jewels.

Now, when this seemingly wicked event took place in Newtown and all those innocent lives were taken, I remembered the gift of seeing the old Souls of those few children who had come to me. I had no doubt as to why this tragic killing spree had taken place. Those children were but a few of those spiritual volunteers who live among us. It is sad indeed that now their parents have to fight to help "right" this "wrong" as far as gun control is concerned. But, here again, there are no accidents in the Universe. These parents are special people who even amidst their overwhelming grief know what they have to do.

My firm belief is that those children from Newtown were a part of the master plan to help save us from our own innate greed and insatiable hunger for power. Senseless killing and other violent acts happen in this country every day (not to mention the rest of the world), and pitifully we have become immune in our reactions to same. We have become like robots. But when children are senselessly murdered? How could the strongest medicine we could take anesthetize us from the feelings of shock, guilt, anger, and pain? It took this diabolical act to awaken people from their self-induced coma to the power of violence. Why did it happen? It happened because these children (old Souls) had *volunteered* to "play this part" in an all-out effort to awaken humanity to the terrible things we are doing to ourselves. At the risk of sounding like a Bible-thumping preacher, just as Christ volunteered to be crucified in order to save humanity, these children sacrificed themselves for the same reason. I suspect there are thousands of children in this world who have returned because of their selfless love for this planet and humanity.

Now for that dream interpretation.

The first symbol that stands out is the color white: a combination of all colors. White stands for purity, love, innocence. White was worn by the Essenes, virgin brides, nuns with their white headdresses. The feelings/emotions of the dreamer were coming from a place within that was Pure Love. The dreamer was full of unselfish love for her fellow people.

She was sitting on a white beach. The ocean is our spiritual power—a human, tangible image of who we are. The ocean represents our self-empowerment. She was being reminded of her own power.

She was sitting on a "white bench." She was sitting at the edge of her own pure emotions and strength of spirit.

The family "of different races" was playing on the beach. We are all God's children regardless of our creed or color of skin. The Mother image is nurturing and playful, security and self-worth, self-sacrificing for her young. This is combined with the Father and all the boys (male energy). Like yin and yang both male and female energy are needed to balance the human condition. The oldest male child was conversing with the dreamer. This image is an aspect of herself; her male energy that is the warrior, strength, fearless, guardian of the family unit. The practical (male) side of her Self was concerned about his siblings "lack of family orientation." In her daily life she is fearful for the outcome of humanity. But, she (female) answers the young man by reassuring him that "as they mature they will learn what family means." Every single human being is a part of the *whole family*. She is hopeful and confident that humanity will learn to love their brothers and sisters after they grow up!

The children of Connecticut were/are a part of the "family" unit and, as such, have played the "role" of this lifetime that they chose to play. It may not be much of a consolation for those loved ones they left behind, especially the parents who suffer the pain of loss, but the Spirit of those children was mature beyond their years. They have returned to "play on the beach" of their Soul Source.

The end of this dream is awesome. She doesn't want to see them leave. She doesn't want to feel the pain of their leaving. None of us did. We all mourned their passing. She closes her eyes, but they are still there when she opens them. Their memory will stay forever, regardless. The child holds out his hand to her and gives her a deep bow. The family line up and also bow so she returns the honor.

This is a validation for all people that the Soul never dies and these children will remain alive with each one of us who is left behind. You may or may not know of the custom of the Eastern religions whereby people honor each other by bowing in greeting or farewell and saying the word "Namaste." Do you know what Namaste means?

*NAMASTE: I honor the place in you in which
the entire universe dwells.*

*I honor the place in you which is of love, of truth,
of life and of peace.*

*When you are in that place in you and I am in
that place in me we are One.*

What a gift this dreamer was given! She asked for
help, and she received help and more. She received Pure
Love. For you dear reader, I hope this story will remind
you of who you really are. For the parents of the Newtown children and those teachers that volunteered to
accompany them through their transition, I can only
honor them by repeating a heartfelt Namaste.

Since meeting these children who are old Souls, I'm
more aware of seemingly ordinary children with whom I
come in contact. While visiting a client who had invited
me to give a workshop at her home, I had the privilege of
meeting one of these old Souls in the guise of her twelve-
year-old son. The young man was so polite and tenta-
tively said, "May I ask you a question?" He proceeded to
tell me his story. "I was lying in bed and had this dream,
but think it was really a vision. I saw myself hovering
above the bed looking down at my body. Could I have
been experiencing a past life?" All I could answer was
"yes." How could I explain to a twelve-year-old that he
was so evolved he was capable of detaching his spirit from
the body like a yogi so he could view himself having a
human experience? He truly knows that we are spirit,
mind, and body and not the other way around, as most
of us view our earthly existence. At such a tender age,
he's not yet aware of who he really is, but I suspect he's

destined to be one of those volunteers that will help turn our world back on its right axis.

I have an eight-year-old granddaughter who is very smart, manipulative, and materialistic. Of course, she is well loved too. She proclaimed to me that "I love my dreams, Nana, because in them I'm always rich!" As she obviously takes her dreams seriously, there is hope for her yet!

When asking for help via your dreams, don't be disappointed if you don't receive an answer immediately. Remember that time as we know it is a man-made concept and the Spirit world is timeless. If you really want to boggle your mind, think about the fact that *everything is happening right now simultaneously*. Einstein proved that there is no such thing as "time." (But that's a whole different subject and one that I'm not going to go into.) Anyway, be patient when asking for help and continue to focus on your request. If what you're asking is something that is in your own best interest, you'll be given the answer.

As far back as biblical times there are stories of characters asking for help and being sent the answer to their problem in the form of a dream. What always seems amazing to me when reading these stories is that the people who received the dreams were so accepting of this phenomenon.

They never seemed to be skeptical of the content or fearful of the deliverer of the dream. They just accepted the message without question and followed its direction explicitly. It makes me wonder why the majority of our present "civilized" culture considers the dream-world to be meaningless gibberish. Are we really so civilized now, or did our distant ancestors have more sophisticated knowledge that we've lost over the centuries?

Asking for help with problems that are stumping you is as easy as learning your ABCs. All you have to do is to quit worrying over the problem, throw your hands in the air, and *let go*. Step out of the way of yourself (I mean you, ego!) and allow your subconscious to take over. As proven by my dream of finding my ring, even if you don't always remember your dream the answer will be given to you.

Even if you still think you never dream; that's okay. Your subconscious doesn't care because it's programmed to assist you anyway. As long as you're willing to let go and allow it to work for you, you'll *remember*. You don't have to be conscious of assembling the parts correctly on the "conveyor belt," but you do have to turn the switch on in order for the belt to move.

Recap

Acceptance of the "unseen" world is a must when asking for help via dreams. Keep it simple when asking for help. Trying too hard is only going to create "mixed signals." Relax! Let go and let God.

Denial is a big obstacle to communicating via your dream-state. Trust is a must.

Sometimes you may not remember the dream, but that doesn't mean that your subconscious hasn't been working while you've been asleep. On awakening you will more than likely have the answer to the problem regardless of what you remember about your dreams.

Fear and skepticism have no place in learning to ask your dreams for answers. "Trust and let go" is a powerful mantra.

Remember that time is a man-made concept and realize that your dream answer may not always appear immediately following your request.

Regardless of whether or not you believe you dream, or don't remember dreaming, your subconscious is still producing them.

≈ 6 ≈

Precognitive Dreams

Dreams are not a New Age discovery. This is especially true with regard to precognitive dreaming. Since time immemorial, thousands of people have experienced such phenomena. Famous people have had precognitive dreams as well as just your next door neighbor. Personally I've had precognitive dreams for as long as I can remember, and having been reared in a family environment that encouraged delving into the paranormal, I grew up thinking that everyone else did too. It wasn't until I reached adulthood that I realized that there were people who claimed not to dream, period, never mind having those of a precognitive nature. I learned to keep such experiences to myself when my claims were not always met by a positive reaction as an adult.

Hopefully, by this time you are convinced that dreams are a vital part of who you are. And they have been around since the beginning of time as we know it. The person who has precognitive dreams carries the burden of deciding whether or not you can alter future events. Usually you can't.

So what can you do when you have a precognitive dream? If it's a warning of an event that may affect someone's life and you can help by telling them, then do so. Whether or not they choose to listen to you is up to them. Don't feel bad if they ignore the warning and the event comes to pass. Remember you can't invade another person's will. If the warning dream is about a national event, it's even more difficult to tell it to a mass of people! Everyone knows that for years nations have been warned about global warming with *physical* evidence. Yet even so, very little has been accomplished to stop the problem. If one, insignificant John or Jane Doe has a precognitive dream that forewarns a rising of the seas that will swallow up cities, who is going to take heed? If people don't want to hear about negative physical evidence, they are not going to want to pay attention to some "crackpot" predicting metaphysical doom and gloom!

But all precognitive dreams are not foreboding Armageddon. Sometimes you may have a precognitive dream of a joyful event, in which case you can just say "thank you" to your subconscious and prepare for the fun occasion. Precognitive dreaming can be a blessing or a curse but, in either case, use the gift wisely.

As I've said, dreaming of future events isn't a modern discovery. The Bible records prophetic dreams as far back as Genesis, starting with Adam. Unfortunately the Bible is somewhat vague on timelines and specific dates, but the Sumerians who flourished 4,000 years ago were not only the inventors of writing, they also recorded incidences of precognitive dreams. The Judeo-Christian "Good Book" is full of characters having precognitive dreams; the most famous being Joseph that prolific dreamer who warned Egypt of the plagues it would endure after having been told so via his dreams. He's the one with the coat of many colors.

Closer to home and according to some historians, Abraham Lincoln had a repeated dream that told of his own death. Apparently this metaphysically minded man took his dreams seriously and talked about them with those close to him. In his biography by Carl Sandberg, he is quoted as saying: "It seems strange how much there is in the Bible about dreams.[. . .] If we believe the Bible we must accept the fact that in the old days God and his angels came to them in their sleep and made themselves known in dreams."

In more recent history, we had Jeanne Dixon of Washington, DC. As a Washington columnist as well as a gifted psychic, she had precognitive dreams. The most well-known dream that threw her into the limelight was the one that foretold John Kennedy's death. Apparently she claimed that she tried to get a warning to him through people she knew at the White House. So who is going to have the guts to tell the president that a psychic says he's about to meet his Maker? In her autobiography *Gift of Prophecy*—an eye-opening read—she says that at his funeral cortege she observed his "ghost" dancing a jig on his coffin.

During the mid-1940s, President Roosevelt called Dixon to the White House. He was very ill at that time, and apparently he asked her how much more time he had before he died—and she told him. Her autobiography is a fascinating story of a truly gifted psychic who really worked with her precognitive dreams.

At the turn of the 19th century, Carl Jung and Sigmund Freud brought dreams to the public's attention by showing their importance relating to the healing of the human psyche. They realized how important dreams were for a person's emotional and mental health, and they used them in their clinical studies. Jung's book *Memories, Dreams, Reflections* is a great example of how dreams have been utilized in the field of psychology. Since that time many of their counterparts have used dream images in their healing work.

But it was Edgar Cayce, the eminent psychic, who brought dreaming to the attention of the general public. In many of his healing sessions for clients, Cayce would interpret their dreams, and from understanding what they were advising, he would guide the client accordingly. His gifted knowledge and expertise really helped awaken the world to the importance of the dream-world. To this day, his symbols and explanations are used in dream interpretation, and most dream dictionaries are based on his symbols. Where did Cayce come by his gifted knowledge? Where else could it have come from but his subconscious? Naturally I'm convinced that this wasn't the first lifetime in which he'd used his gifts.

But even Cayce cautioned people not to depend completely on generalized symbols. He advocated developing your own symbolism, and I definitely feel the same. For example, over the years I've learned that whenever I dream of a brand-new baby, it means that something new is about to enter my life; changes are about to take place. I look at the "story" and again—very important— I remember my *feelings* during the dream. Whatever the "baby" is telling me is what changes are about to happen and the area of my life I need to pay attention to. Develop your own symbols according to what they mean to you, and only you. This also applies to precognitive dreams.

Whenever I have a precognitive dream, it is usually related to events within my circle of family and close friends. The one time a dream deviated from this tendency was during the 1980s when I had a dream about the airplane disaster over Lockheed, Scotland. The dream came to me approximately one week before the tragedy, and although I didn't know where it was going to take place, it showed me the event. In the dream I was trying desperately to *will* the plane to stay in the air. My feelings were very anxious and desperate. I can only hazard a guess that the reason this seemingly unconnected, precognitive dream came to me is because there may have been someone who was on that plane that I had known during my life and with whom I'd lost contact over the years. We all have this happen to us. We are close to someone, and then our lives take different paths and we lose touch with each other. Yes, dreams that foretell the future can be burdensome when there is nothing you can do to stop the event, but I've learned that what is meant to be will be and it's not for me to question why.

If you have precognitive dreams and don't know how to handle them, as I've said already, look at your *feelings* during the story. If it's a negative event that can possibly be alleviated by your intervention, do what you can, but please realize that you cannot change another person's will. If the event cannot be changed, thank the Universe for giving you this gift of foresight and bless the future happening and hope that goodwill will lessen the impact. Always thank the Universe for giving you this type of dream. Pray that the event may have a positive outcome, and if it doesn't, know that whatever is meant to be will be.

Here is a personal example of what I mean. I had a dream concerning a friend of mine who lived in another state. In the dream she was telling me that she was about to pay me a surprise visit. During the conversation she revealed that she'd been having pains in her legs and didn't know what to do about it. In the dream I was telling her that she had high blood pressure.

The following day I actually received a telephone call from this friend, and she told me that her employer was sending her to Oregon on a business trip and she naturally would be visiting me. When I told her about the dream, she laughed and said "You and your dreams!" Then, she admitted that she indeed had painful legs. I have to add that this friend was only five foot two inches and carried too much weight for her height. Needless to say, she heeded my dream warning, sought out her doctor, and he confirmed that her blood pressure was elevated. Thank goodness that this doctor was thorough in his examination and checked for blood clots. Luckily none were found, and I sighed with relief. This is one instance when a precognitive dream can avert a possible problem.

If the dream does use symbols to tell you a future event and you don't understand what it's trying to share, before going to sleep ask for another dream that will give you more clarity. I cannot emphasize this enough. Remember to keep it simple and trust that you'll get the answer. Usually a precognitive dream is already very simple and factual so that the interpretation is very clear. I must reiterate that it's important to remember that you can't always alter the events, so don't think that you can. You're not God, and the only person you can control is *yourself*.

Recap

Precognitive dreams have been around since time immemorial and are not unique to this century. From the Bible to Abraham Lincoln into the 20th century with the emergence of Edgar Cayce and on to Jeanne Dixon and beyond, this type of dreaming is a normal part of some people's psyche.

Most of the time the recipient of a precognitive dream cannot change "future" events, and this can become a burden if you let it be so. Realizing that you're not God and only have control of your own actions can keep you balanced. Always remember this.

In some instances a dream of this nature can be an asset for your own well-being or another person's, but only if you (or that other person) are willing to listen and act upon the dream's message.

Precognitive dreams are usually very clear and need no clarification, but as with all dreams, ask for more help if you don't get the message the first time.

Use precognitive dreams with discretion and respect, according to the scenario you have been given. Always thank the Universe for the gift of this type of dream.

≈ 7 ≈

Relationships

Ah, those dynamic relationship problems! Relationships are always a "biggy" whether it's a relationship with a family member, best friend, coworker, or—the crème de la crème of relationships—your marriage partner or significant other. Life's lessons are all about connecting and interacting with each other because that's what life is all about. Whether it is a massive interaction that impacts humankind, such as worldwide wars, or a single connection with your neighbor, relationships are the cause and effect of this planet's existence. Having said all that, I'm going to concentrate here on your own personal relationships and leave the worldwide "karmic lessons" for another and much wiser person than yours truly.

You are having problems with your partner and have tried every means possible to resolve the issue. Nothing you're doing is working. This is when your subconscious will step in and take over. It will use your dream-time to advise you as to what actions you must take to overcome the difficulty. But, beware, you may not always like the answer. Regardless, your subconscious is working only for *your* best interests and not the other person's. A dream may be telling you to move on and leave the relationship behind. The lesson may be over for you even if the partner's "role" is not completely finished. That's your partner's problem, not yours, and beating a dead horse is a waste of energy.

To ignore a dream that is clearly telling you to break away from the relationship only prolongs the agony. This is when we are allowing the ego to take over. Contrary to popular belief, there's nothing wrong with having an ego. It's a necessary part of who we are. It's when you allow the ego to become egotistical that the trouble starts.

Unfortunately we are all masochists at various times in our lives and enjoy the pain too much to let go of the problem that is causing the pain! Dragging the situation along as if you're lugging a fifty-pound sack of spuds is not conducive to your well-being. What happens if you have a bad tooth and you are too chicken to see a dentist? Eventually if you neglect the bad tooth for too long a time, instead of only needing a filling, you eventually have to submit to a root canal. Ooch! And so, if you ignore a warning dream that is pointing out that a relationship in your life is detrimental to your overall health, it will keep nagging you with repeated messages until you take notice. Your subconscious is a great taskmaster and hangs in there like a pitbull. The situation isn't going to go away even if you ignore the warning dreams. And the relationship may deteriorate from just being an uncomfortable ache to a full-blown "abscessed tooth."

I know it's hard to step back and become detached while in a close relationship that's broken down, but you have to do this. Therefore, this is a good time to practice taking a trip to your own personal "theater" and sitting in the audience to watch your "play." This visualization is a great way to allow your mind to detach. Seeing the problem from the perspective of an "audience" rather than being involved in the drama onstage, gives you clearer insights about the role you are playing with the other person.

Imagine you're sitting in your theater audience watching players on the stage acting their parts. The players are fighting a duel. Of course, you know it's just the roles they have chosen to play; they mean no harm to each other in reality. Or do they?

Observing them as an audience member, you may critique their acting ability. What are your *feelings* about their performances? Are they overacting, enjoying their roles, too aggressive and in danger of killing each other, or just playing at sparring in order to get a rise out of the opponent? Are you watching them with a sense of irritation or excitement or boredom or anger or fright, or are you sitting back and thoroughly enjoying the conflict that's going on? Do you realize that the players are aspects of *you and your relationship with yourself?*

Once you've watched these two people as an observer without the entanglement of being a participant, then be aware of your feelings. You may be surprised at the emotions you're experiencing. After you've gone through analyzing this personal experience with detached honesty, you're ready to receive some really honest answers. When you go to sleep that night, ask your subconscious for a solution. Of course, the ideal time to go through this exercise is before you go to bed, but if this isn't possible, that's still okay because the insights you will have gleaned from your visual playacting will stay with you regardless. You've prepared yourself to look at your dreams with a detached, nonpersonalized attitude.

Here again is one of my own examples regarding a relationship problem and a dream's warning. The night before I was to marry my first husband, I had the following dream. *My mother was with me, and she was crying as she watched my preparations to marry.* That was the whole extent of the dream. It was all I needed because the *feelings* were overwhelming. I experienced sorrow and a tremendous sense of foreboding. It didn't take a rocket scientist to get the message; it was loud and clear. However, being only a few hours away from the altar and believing that it was too late to back out, I rationalized that I couldn't just cancel everything. I chose to ignore the warning. In other words, I was allowing my ego to be egotistical. Ah me, the foolishness of youth!

Needless to say, I spent too long a time in a marriage that was not merely a miserable headache but a full-blown migraine. Of course, there are no such things as accidents, and this marriage was a lesson meant for my personal growth. But could I have learned the same lesson by taking an easier road? I think so. The dream was obviously warning of the sorrow and pain I was about to reap and was giving me an opportunity to back out before it was too late. It was showing me the path I was about to embark on and giving me the chance to change it if I chose to do so. I probably could have taken a less painful route for my Soul's development, but because we have free will, even your subconscious can't interfere with your conscious decisions. I have to confess that I'm a Capricorn (sign of the goat), which means I feel the need to plod up the mountainside instead of taking a fun ski lift to the top! Obviously I felt it necessary to have to scramble over treacherous rocks and climb steep cliffs in my attempt to scale my spiritual "Mount Everest."

The same holds true for any relationship. If you need to make a decision regarding career and/or working entanglements that could be a mistake, you know what to do, don't you? *Heed your dreams.* You can guarantee that your subconscious will attempt to stop you from tripping up. The dream may be warning you of a small incident that could possibly cause you embarrassment in the workplace or a bigger blunder that could get you fired. Regardless of the size, your subconscious will try to protect you ahead of time by sending you a warning via your dreams. The same holds true in any close relationship. If you have a parental problem or a jealous sibling who has you feeling as if your back is against a wall, when all else has failed, then ask for help through your dream-guidance. You may not be able to change this person's attitude toward you, but the dream will show you how to change your own attitude toward solving the problem by looking *within yourself.*

We are not left to stumble blindly in the dark not knowing where we are going. Whether it's your work environment, a sibling rivalry, a close friendship gone haywire, parental problems, or that intimate relationship with your significant other, ask for help and you'll get it. We may be in the dark, but our subconscious is not. Our dreams will not only provide a lamp to light our way but will take our hand and lead us out of the darkness. And, if you get a dream response you don't understand, what do you do? You've got it! Ask for clarification via another dream.

Following are more personal examples of what I'm talking about.

> *I was struggling to climb a mountain (Capricorn goat again) and stumbling over boulders and crevices. All at once, I noticed that "around the corner" of the mountain was a perfectly smooth path with folks hiking up the mountainside without any difficulty.*

The problem that I was having at that particular time wasn't as hard to solve as I'd thought. I was trying too hard and ignoring the obvious solution. I found an easier "path" to climb through the problem.

> I was in a house next to a river, and the river was flooding its banks. The water was rising, and I felt it lapping against my ankles, so I ascended to the highest floor of the house to escape the danger.

Puzzling over the dream and the symbols it had provided, I really couldn't determine what warning it was giving to me. Yet because of my *feelings*, I knew it was a warning dream. The next night before I went to sleep, I asked for more clarity.

> I was watching two youngsters swimming, and one of them was in trouble. The other one was having difficulty in trying to save the first from drowning. Feeling very anxious, I dashed frantically to their assistance.

We'll get into commonly used symbols later but in general, water is a symbol of your life source. It's your sustenance. You can't live without water, because the body is predominantly made up of fluid. In dreams water also represents your spiritual power, emotions, the Soul's journey.

So, what was happening in the two dreams? A: I was in danger of being "flooded" and overtaken by the rising waters. B: I was watching someone drown and frantically trying to save this child.

In both dreams the predominant feeling was anxiety.

As I have said, in most cases characters in your dreams are an aspect of yourself. Therefore the first dream was telling me that I was in danger of getting "flooded" out of my "home" (my security), and I was seeking higher ground (Higher Consciousness) to protect myself. In the second dream I was in danger of drowning (water again) and was trying to save myself. Was my life in danger either physically or spiritually?

At this particular time in my life I was in fact "flooding" myself with too many responsibilities. I was stretching myself to the ultimate limit physically, mentally, and spiritually. Without realizing it, I was in danger of exhausting my energy, damaging my health, and consequently "drowning." My spiritual journey was in jeopardy because I wasn't taking care of my physical being. The dreams were my subconscious telling me to slow down and remember who I am. I am still a spirit having a human experience, but unless I take care of my health, my body will not be capable of continuing to "house" my spirit, and I'll "drown." I had enough sense to pay a visit to my doctor.

Your Higher Consciousness is always guiding your life, whether you know it or not. Consider a director of a play or movie. A good one will guide the actor through a role in such a way as to get the best performance out of him or her. The director takes each part of the individual portrayed and coaches the performer according to that unique personal role. Just as a puppeteer guides the strings of a puppet, the director guides the players to bring forth all of the abilities that they are capable of in order for them to give a brilliant performance. The director tells them how to use body language, phrase and pronounce their lines with conviction, and move their body in a certain direction. In other words, the director guides them in an attempt to make their performance the greatest. Believe it or not, even Meryl Streep or a legend like the late Sir Laurence Olivier needs a good director.

Your subconscious is your personal director, and your dreams are the guidance it gives you. Dreams help you to play out your "life's role" to its ultimate best so that you may give your most outstanding performance.

Recap

Relationships are what makes the world go around. When we make a mess of our relationships, the subconscious will bend over backward via dreams to straighten out the problem for us.

You may not always like the answer it gives to relationship problems, but your subconscious is all about *your* welfare and not anyone else's karmic lessons.

Even if you don't like to look at negative aspects of yourself, you have to be honest and face whatever demons you are carrying within yourself that are creating the relationship problem you are experiencing. I'm not saying that your partner is "right" and you are "wrong." What I am saying is to ask yourself why you have chosen to create this bad situation in your life. Why do you gravitate to being abused emotionally, mentally, or physically? What are you lacking in self-esteem that allows you to feel downtrodden or betrayed? Your dreams will help you to find the answer, but you have to be open to accepting the truth. Like the Snow White mirror, you can't lie to yourself as your dreams, as a part of yourself, mirror your psyche.

Remember, you're not alone. Ask for help. Allow your dreams to unfold, and then follow the "road" they are telling you to take. *Listen* and *learn*.

Learn detachment when looking at the problem relationship. This will help you to get answers. Visualize yourself in that personal theater watching the players on the stage with a detached attitude.

Be willing to acknowledge your dream's message if it's telling you that *you* are the problem. By the same token, if it's telling you to get out of a bad situation: do it!

⮞ 8 ⮜

Literal versus Metaphorical

One dream might cover various aspects of your life all at once in order to help you with multiple stumbling blocks you might be encountering. And so one dream may be literally telling it to you "like it is" as well as giving you a metaphorical message. Being the "show me" person that I am, I'll use a personal dream to explain what I mean.

Over a period of a few weeks I had the same dream on a consistent basis. Obviously, I knew that they were all warning dreams and were faithfully attempting to get my waking attention. The dreams' message was trying to make me aware of something that I needed to avoid and the basics were the same in every dream. *I had lost my purse. It was gone, and I was frantically searching for it.* Naturally I felt very anxious during the dreams, and in one of them was extremely concerned because my credit cards were in the purse. In every dream I felt frustration and awakened with a sense of anxiety. It was definitely not a good way to start the day! I explored all the metaphorical symbols of the dream but could not figure out anything conclusive or reach a satisfactory answer. What was I in danger of losing?

Now I know that most men would say that a woman's purse is so full of junk that it's a miracle we can find anything when we need it. But, apart from the usual clutter, my purse also contained everything that I practically own to keep my life in order.

In dream symbolism a purse is associated with our security or identity. The purse holds our material resources, ideas, and attitudes. A man might dream instead of his wallet—same thing, without the clutter.

So in analyzing this repetitive dream I attempted to discern where I was losing my sense of security, maybe even my identity. What about losing my credit cards? Was I in danger of losing my credibility in any area of my life? My purse contained my driver's license. Was my identity about to be compromised? Car keys, lipstick, checkbook—what was I in danger of losing and what did it signify? Finally the dreams stopped. Even the subconscious will throw in the towel if, like yours truly, you're being too thickheaded to figure out the warning!

Shortly thereafter I had to travel out of state to give a weekend seminar. It was a holiday weekend and most folks had left the major roadways to spend their time away from the cities. The traffic on the major highway wasn't heavy, and the trip went smoothly. Returning home at the end of the weekend, I stopped to fill my car with gas, then continued on my merry way. Arriving home, I relaxed in my favorite armchair and was enjoying a good cup of tea. Then my telephone rang. It was my oldest daughter. "Mom do you have your purse?" What? I hadn't even missed it!

Apparently I had lain it down by the gas pump as I filled up my tank and drove off without it. Luckily an honest person had turned it in to the gas station attendant, and as my daughter's cell phone number was in it, the attendant had called and left a message. But the message was distorted, and we couldn't decipher the return phone number that was left on her answering machine.

In my own defense for my carelessness, I have to say that in the state of Oregon where I live, we don't have to pump our own gas and can sit comfortably in our car while an attendant does the honors. So I'm not familiar with having to go into the station and pay before pumping the gas or using a credit card at the pump. Because I was paying with cash, I had to go inside to the counter. Hence, after prepaying the attendant, I had set the purse down while pumping the gas and then blithely driven away.

To cut a long story short, after many phone calls and much detective work, I finally found that the purse had been handed in to the police department of the town where the gas station was. But this wasn't the end of my problems. Because of the holiday weekend, the business offices of the police station were closed. I had to wait two days before they reopened for business and I could go to their Lost Property department and retrieve the purse. It was also almost a three-hour trip back to the location and needless to say another three hours to return home. Regardless of the amount of stress I endured over the situation and the endless time consumed in phone calls and traveling, I was just thankful that everything inside my purse was intact, including credit cards and cash. Naturally, I thanked my Head Honchos (guides) profusely for watching over my property. Obviously the Spirit world doesn't take off for holidays, for which I'm profoundly grateful.

Yes, I immediately thought of the dreams. They were *literally* telling me that I was about to lose my purse if I didn't take heed! Dah! But wait—there's more. This wasn't the only warning that the dreams were trying to convey, as I later learned.

Shortly after this incident I was involved in a public event that impacted my credibility as an intuitive. Without going into the personal details of the unexpected scenario that evolved, I was invited to appear as a guest on a live-broadcast television talk show, and something took place that left me with the uncomfortable feeling that I was in danger of losing my purpose as a past-life facilitator helping people who are stuck in their personal lives. I was left feeling like an old-time fortune-teller at a carnival sideshow. This incident made me realize that I was slipping into the dangerous place of dishonoring my gift by allowing it to be coopted for its entertainment value. I had the uncomfortable feeling that I was prostituting myself.

The television personnel from the program were completely innocent of causing my discomfort and had no idea as to my feelings. Their intentions were well meant, and everyone treated me with genuine warmth and respect. And, most important, the audience seemed to enjoy the show. Nevertheless, I knew what was happening. Hence the dreams' attention to the danger of "losing my purse" was also telling me *metaphorically* that I was in danger of losing perspective with my psychic gift. I was in danger of not only losing my "identity" (security in who I am) but also my "credibility" (credit cards).

The dreams that you receive are always very thorough, and they don't play around with "soft shoeing" the truth. They tell you exactly what you need to know for your own well-being. And one needs to look at all the aspects of a dream as the messages are more often than not multidimensional. You need to look at a dream from both the literal perspective and the metaphorical. Obviously, if a dream repeats itself, you would be wise to heed its warning and take the right action to avoid a problem.

Ever since this experience—especially if I cannot figure out a dream's message—I am extra cautious in how I walk my daily life. If I'm in a situation that is unfamiliar to me, I'm more careful of my words and actions. The moral of this story is to look at all the aspects of the dream and think before you act. If it's obviously a warning dream and you don't understand it, do like President Truman was supposed to have said: "Walk softly and carry a big stick." Caution is the keyword.

This dream of my lost purse perfectly illustrates what I call the many "facets" of dreams. Don't fall into the trap of trying too hard to figure out the symbolic meaning of the dream. When the warning needs to show you a clear and precise message, *it will do just that.* How? By repeating the same "dialogue" over and over again. Remember to look at all the angles when deciphering the message—literally as well as metaphorically. Obviously, that was one time when I didn't take my own advice!

A dream dictionary can be a big help to you in figuring out the particular meaning of a symbol. I have several of them myself, but you need to be discerning. Don't take the interpretation as verbatim for your particular situation. Dream dictionaries are not meant to replace your own personal symbols and interpretations. Relying completely on a dictionary is like reading your daily horoscope in the newspaper and taking a particular astrological sign as literally meant for you. As you know, each astrological sign covers millions of people and can't possibly be perfectly tailored to your individual journey.

Just as there is much more to astrology and the place, time, and year that you were born than what you get in the newspaper, so it is with all the intricacies of dreams. What may be one symbol for one person may have an entirely different meaning to another. A dog, for example, is generically viewed as a symbol of loyalty, but if you are afraid of dogs, dreaming of one may have threatening connotations for you.

If you don't understand the dream and its symbols, then again I can only emphasize that you ask for clarification.

As with any type of dream, but especially if it's repetitive, you need to take one step at a time in figuring out what it's trying to tell you.

First, be aware of your feelings during the dream. Second, what is going on in your life? How does your present reality relate to the dream? Third, take each symbol in order of importance and analyze how it fits in with your lifestyle and/or situation. And last but not least, consider the dream from a literal perspective as well as a symbolic one.

Recap

Dreams can be literally telling you of an event that might happen (especially warning dreams) as well as conveying a metaphorical message.

If a dream repeats itself, take heed. Pay attention to what the message is that you're not getting. Dreams are extremely thorough and will not miss a single item that needs to be addressed.

Using a dream dictionary can be helpful but don't overdo it and think that what you read is the only interpretation of a symbol as it relates to you.

Analyze your dream systematically, just as you would when balancing your checkbook, starting with how you feel during your dream.

If a dream repeats and repeats and you still can't figure out the warning, then caution in your daily actions is a must. Look before you leap in anything you do.

∼ 9 ∼

Your Health and Dreams

Dreams concerning one's health can be vitally important. They have even been known to save lives, as the following story will attest.

Several years ago I read the autobiography of Wanda Burch in her book *She Who Dreams*. Wanda was raised in one of the southern states and was influenced greatly by her grandmother, who, if I remember correctly, was of Irish descent. Each morning at breakfast they had a ritual of sharing the previous night's dreams, and the grandmother taught the child how to interpret the symbols. Wanda would relate her dream, and the grandmother would help her to understand what it was telling her. Lucky child! Naturally, she grew up respecting and honoring what her dreams conveyed.

During her adult years, Wanda had a repetitive dream that was telling her that she had breast cancer. Consequently, she underwent numerous medical tests that all came back negative. But the dreams continued, and so she became persistent in seeking medical help to confirm what they were saying. Her persistence and faith paid off as eventually the cancer was discovered. Then her dreams began to tell her what she must do to cure the disease.

Amazingly, she found a doctor who actually *listened and also believed her dreams*! Along with known medical treatments, this farsighted doctor used the healing techniques that Wanda's dreams instructed him to use. Eventually, the breast cancer disappeared.

She Who Dreams is well worth reading for anyone needing validation for the power of dreams, not to mention anyone suffering from a life-threatening illness.

~

Although Wanda's story is compelling, it isn't enough to heal yourself physically. Whatever the physical ailment is, it's more often than not the outcome of a long-standing emotional or mental ailment. Getting rid of a headache with an aspirin isn't always the "cure." It would be as if a doctor prescribed an analgesic for a head pain that might be an indication of a brain tumor instead. If an emotional or mental problem is causing your "pain," a dream will usually tell you what the real problem is and how to heal it. Wonder of wonders, your dreams will even tell you of a health problem before you or your doctor is aware of it! Of course, if you don't heed the dream's warning—even if it's repeated—it won't do you any good. The dream can be the UPS guy who delivers a box to your door, but you still have to open it up and see what's inside . . .

The world of medicine is opening up to the fact that there is more to healing than dispensing a pill for a specific ailment. Thanks to people such as Deepak Chopra and Bernie Siegel—to name just two—medical practitioners have learned that healing just the physical body isn't going to cut it. Doctors are finally taking into consideration that physical afflictions may be caused by psychological or emotional events that have traumatized a patient. They are especially looking at people who suffer from asthma, as this condition could possibly be caused by a stressful situation in the person's life. Even more significant is that at a deeper subconscious level, a patient may have incarnated with a serious problem from a former life. If this is the case, your subconscious will bend over backward to show you by allowing you to revisit the "past" during your sleep.

From my many years of having the privilege of "seeing" clients' past lives, I know that we frequently return still carrying the effects of a previous traumatic experience. As one example, I saw a client who had lived as a "trailblazer" on the Great Plains when this country was still mostly uninhabited by the European immigrants. During that life he had caught a foot in one of his animal traps and "died" an agonizing death due to gangrene infecting the wound. In this present life he admitted to having painful problems with his legs and feet.

Another person had spent a life during the Spanish Inquisition, when he'd been imprisoned for five years in a small cell before he finally succumbed to death. This person now suffers from claustrophobia (fear of closed spaces). Another client had led a life as a tracker in the wilderness of Canada. The male incarnation had broken his leg far from civilization and therefore had to set it himself. He walked with a limp for the rest of his life, and I suspect it continued to be painful. In his current life as a woman, there had been a bad car accident, and she had had a steel rod placed in a leg to hold it together.

Many people dream of past-life traumas and/or health issues without knowing that they are doing so. When such dreams occur, your subconscious is trying to help you heal the wound that you've carried into your "present" existence. I have to say that the reason it's hard to cure a past-life wound is that we don't always want to go there again so will bury it deeply in our memory bank. Usually such a dream is passed off as a nightmare by our conscious mind. Regardless, the subconscious will bring it forth because the trauma needs to be resolved. Knowing where a health problem originated will certainly aid in its cure.

Facing the facts of the dream and realizing that these facts are hampering your personal growth are a big step toward healing the problem. Your subconscious hasn't forgotten. Anyone who has read Brian Weiss's book *Many Lives, Many Masters* will attest to the fact that traumas from past lives do continue to haunt our present existence. Whether your health issue has manifested during this lifetime or a past trauma, your dreams will go 99 percent of the way to help in the healing process. All you have to do is to go the remaining 10 percent by listening and learning. And if you don't understand a dream that your gut instinct is telling you to note, then ask for another dream that will clarify it further for you. "Ask and it will be given to you; seek, and you will find." This isn't just an enigmatic biblical quote. It's fact. Keep it simple. There's nothing complicated about dreams—unless you make them complicated.

A common symbol of a health issue, whether physical, mental, or spiritual, is dreaming of a car as you'll recall from our exploration of Joan's past life as an Indian. The car signifies your body transporting you through life. The following is a very simplistic example of a dream giving you messages concerning your health: *Your car's headlights aren't working, or you're driving in a fog and unable to see the road clearly.* Such a dream can have more than one message for you. Headlights not working could be that your eyesight is poor and you need to seek a professional examination. Driving in a fog could still mean sight problems, but it could also symbolize that you are "in a fog" over some decision that you need to make in your life. You may need to clear your mind in order to see the problem clearly. Whatever function that the car is performing in your dream is symbolic of what is wrong with your health.

If you're in your car and it's sliding backward and out of control, this usually means that some area of your life is out of control—physically, mentally, or emotionally. All three aspects can be detrimental to your health. Consider the various parts of the car and you'll find the related body part, such as Engine = Heart, Tires = Feet, etc. The type of car you are driving can also be indicative of what is going on in your life. A racing car, for example, could mean that you are "driving too fast" or living dangerously. You need to slow down and take stock of your health.

Sometimes it isn't a car that's your transportation/ body in your dreams. I have a friend who worked as a railroad engineer. He spent at least eight hours per day operating trains and much less time driving to work in his car. Consequently his dream body is a train—different images but same concept. Your subconscious adjusts to whatever is easiest for you to understand. It could be a truck driver, taxicab operator, bus driver; whatever vehicle is the most familiar to you will usually signify your body in your dreams. This is one reason that it's important to develop your own symbols.

I once had a dream that I tried to use my car brakes and they felt like mush. My foot was on the brake pedal, and it went all the way to the floorboard. I couldn't figure out the symbolism but knew that an area of my "car" was apparently having a problem. Guess what? Shortly after this dream I was diagnosed with high blood sugar. I needed to take the necessary actions to *bring it under control*. Instead of neglecting to service my brakes and pressing them to the limit (lack of self-control), I needed to stop "breaking" the limits of my bodily endurance. Your subconscious is working to protect you even if you are not. And, most important, just like the woman who had breast cancer, don't forget that the subconscious is aware of a health issue even when you and your doctor are not.

Of course, the clinical study of dreams as related to a person's health has been taking place since the time of Freud and Jung. Many years later during the 1980s, a Dr. Robert Smith at Michigan State University studied cardiac patients and found that those who dreamed of death and destruction suffered from extensive heart damage, even though they weren't always aware of how serious their condition was. If you are interested in knowing more about the psychology of dreams and your health, I suggest you read Freud or Jung.

Personally, I like to keep things simple and feel that dreams adapt to what the recipient can handle and understand. After all, it is your subconscious that's bringing forth the dreams, and therefore you're in control of your brain giving you information in the most comprehensible way for your intellect to handle. I've often wondered about the type of dreams people who suffer from mental challenges such as Down syndrome or Alzheimer's may have.

Naturally, you always have to take into consideration the story line of your dream, and I can't emphasize enough the importance of your emotions during the scenario that is being presented. Are you anxious or joyful? Is fear surrounding you, or are you confident? If you work with and follow the guidance of your dreams, any ailment can be taken care of in a positive manner before it gets out of control. We've already shown this with Wanda's story.

It should go without saying, however, that along with advice from your dreams you need to seek expert medical attention. We have a conscious, commonsense brain as well as a subconscious, and relying completely on one without the other is foolhardy. We live in an age of advanced medical technology as well as an enlightened metaphysical consciousness, so utilize the best of both worlds. As in all things, balance is the keyword.

When looking at your dreams that seem to indicate a health problem, ask yourself questions. Write down the most significant symbol in the dream, whether it is a person, object, animal, or situation. Analyze that symbol and look at your feelings surrounding it. Is it someone you know and is representing an aspect of yourself? Example: Is it someone that you think of as being a hypochondriac and complains all the time? Do you feel exasperated with them and wish they'd stop constantly complaining? Remember, other people appearing in your dream are usually aspects of yourself. Are you dwelling on a health issue too much and blowing it out of proportion? Or is your dream trying to tell you that maybe you're going to the opposite extreme and ignoring a physical or mental problem you should be paying more attention to? Are you out of balance physically, mentally, and/or emotionally?

If the main symbol of the dream is an animal, ask yourself what that animal means to you. Example: If the animal is a fat pig, are you overeating and gaining too much weight? I had a dream that I was lugging around a big, apelike monkey that was clinging to my back. At that particular time I was holding a very long-term resentment toward someone who I perceived had hurt me emotionally. The dream was telling me in no uncertain terms that I needed to get over it and move on. I needed to get rid of that "monkey on my back." Like I've said, dreams don't balk at telling you the truth. There is no subterfuge to your subconscious.

Let's say you dream that you're in a desert and frantically looking for an oasis because you're dying of thirst. Is your body in need of more fluids? Are you having symptoms of a medical ailment that could relate to your kidney function and/or bladder? Or is it a subtler message that you need to be "refreshed" in some area of your mental or emotional life?

These are very simplistic examples, but I'm sure you get the idea. Remember, your subconscious knows what is going on with your health before you do, so take notice.

After you've analyzed the most outstanding symbol in your dream, look at the second symbol that seems to stand out in the story. Cover each symbol in order of importance. Then look at the whole picture and ask yourself, how does this relate to what is going on in my life at this moment?

Is it a health problem that you are somewhat aware of but have the attitude that if you ignore it maybe it will go away? Stop! Your dream is telling you differently, and you need to seek professional advice.

Is it a situation that is puzzling to you? It could be a health issue from your "past," in which case ask for clarification. If it's a dream about a health problem that you are unaware of, then your subconscious usually doesn't play around. It will "tell it like it is" so that you can take the necessary action.

Louise Hay's *You Can Heal Your Life* is a great testament to the power of faith in your subconscious as well as your conscious brain. I don't know whether or not she utilized her dreams in healing herself of her own cancer, but I would like to bet she did. In our world there are many intricate concepts that come under the umbrella of metaphysics, and dreams are an important spoke connected to the hub of the wheel that I like to refer to as the Wheel of Life.

Don't ignore persistent health dreams even if you don't seem to have any symptoms. It could—as was the case with Wanda Burch—be a life-threatening problem. Using awareness in your dreams could save your life, as she testified. Cancer is so insidious that many people who have it don't notice any symptoms until it's too late.

We are living in an age whereby anything we need is available to us for the asking for balancing the body, mind, and spirit. Western civilization has finally caught up with the intuitive knowledge of the East; dreams being just one powerful tool for healing. Australian aborigines and Peruvian Indians, to name just two of the many cultures of the world, have used the dream-world in their healing ceremonies for centuries.

Should you find you have a health issue, then before going to sleep, you can also ask to be healed through your dreams. Visualize yourself as being whole and healthy and keep the thought of healing in your mind until you drop off. Whatever needs healing within your mind or body, see yourself as being pain-free, dancing with joy, breathing and taking air into your lungs to expand them to their fullest capacity. Then let go and allow your subconscious to take over. It may take more than one night but remember that "Rome wasn't built in a day." Patience and persistence are keywords.

Recap

Don't ignore dreams that concern your health. As proof of this fact, consider what Wanda Burch wrote of her own experience with this phenomena in her book *She Who Dreams.*

Don't be hesitant about discussing your dreams of health problems with a doctor, whether you think it is a physical or mental ailment. If your present doctor is too skeptical, change doctors! We are living in an age when physicians are becoming more open to the world of the hidden psyche.

It is quite common for a person to have a health problem from a previous lifetime carry over into the present one. If that's the case for you, it will resurface in your dreams if it still needs to be resolved.

Remember that dreaming about your car is symbolic of your body, your transportation in this life. If there is something wrong with the car, there's usually something physically, emotionally, or mentally not right with your body.

Your body may not always be a car. It depends on what mode of transport you're comfortable with and commonly use in life.

Sometimes your subconscious is aware of a problem before you are. It won't go away by ignoring it.

When "dissecting" your dreams, take one step at a time. Always start with how you are feeling in the dream.

Take the next most significant symbol and digest how it relates to you. Continue with each symbol in order of importance in the dream and finally look at the whole story line and its relationship to your present circumstances.

Last but not least, if you are having a specific health problem, ask for help via your dream-time before retiring for the night. You'll be surprised at what this simple act can do for you.

⌒ 10 ⌒

Lucid Dreaming

A lucid dream is nothing like anything we've ever experienced in our waking reality. In recent years lucid dreaming has been linked to quantum physics, but as my brain operates on a metaphysical level and physics is a foreign language to me, whether I like it or not, I have to take this link on faith. Even so, I can't help but think to myself, "So what else is new?" Our known Universe is full of undiscovered magnificence, and one more discovery of its wonders is as if one were trying to figure out the intricacies of a single snowflake falling on the Himalayas. Isn't the dreamworld as endlessly full of surprises as the Universe?

Having a lucid dream is like taking a vacation to a place you've never visited before, which at the same time feels completely familiar to you. An example is the dream I related in chapter one when I was in outer space and feeling completely at peace with myself and the world. A lucid dream may range from this kind of momentous happening that takes the dreamer through an experience that is beyond words to but a fleeting recognition that he/ she is dreaming.

A lucid dream that I consider to be such a fleeting recognition is a repetitive dream that I have of playing a piano. To explain the background of this dream, I have to go back to my childhood. I began to play the piano by ear when I was about seven years old. My folks ran a pub, and on weekends the main saloon-bar was open for entertainment. One of the customer's would sit at the piano and play all the old favorite songs while all the other patrons sang along with as much gusto as they gulped down their booze. I have to say that even as a child, I knew which stage of inebriation the customers were in by the type of songs they would sing. When they were fully drunk but still capable of understanding, they'd let loose with bawdy songs without any show of inhibition. Eventually when they were no longer feeling any pain, they'd turn to more sentimental fare. I'd listen to them, and when the pub was closed and I had the bar to myself, I would play the songs by picking out the tune on the keys. Of course, I had more sense than to try to figure out the more risqué choices. Unfortunately, my mother, bless her heart, was convinced that she had a musical savant on her hands and decided that I must have music lessons. A relative who had taught himself to read music warned her that if he taught me to read music as she requested I would lose the ability to play by ear and would never be that good at either because of this. He was right. Although I always loved playing, I was far from concert pianist material!

In my dream I'm always playing the piano as exquisitely as if I were an actual part of the instrument. I'm aware of my fingers flying over the keys, and the beautiful music coming forth has a life of its own. I am an indelible part of the keyboard. With no seeming effort I play what I want, and the piano is enriching my Soul. The feeling is oh so familiar. It's as if I'm playing somewhere in my "past." I'm in complete control of the music I'm creating as my fingers move with such ease up and down scales and over flats and sharps. Once again, as in the dream of being in outer space, I'm extremely conscious of the fact that I'm dreaming, which enhances the experience beyond words. All too soon, I am aware that I must return to the confines of my body. My reluctance is profound. Even so, this wondrous feeling of Completeness stays with me throughout my day. I am All That Is. With any lucid dream the dreamer is more than likely to feel reluctant to leave the dream and return to this reality we call life.

The fact that a lucid dreamer can orchestrate the structure of a dream is empowering, but it's not a guarantee that the story line is what the dreamer thinks it might be. It's usually better than you hoped for! When you are experiencing a regular dream, the images you see are sometimes nonsensical because the subconscious is bringing forth subtle messages that relate to the mundane happenings of your daily life as well as more serious issues. Via a lucid dream you may *consciously* explore anything you want and *know* that you are doing so. A lucid dream is always more than three-dimensional and makes perfect sense to the dreamer.

A man recently shared with me a lucid dream he had been having more than once. There was no symbolism, just a straightforward dream that he felt was "self-induced." In the dream, he was preparing to return to his "home" on another planet. Awesome! Although he had never heard of lucid dreaming, he was still conscious of the fact that he was asleep and dreaming. I have seen a few clients' past lives as having been lived on other planets in our Universe and must say that it's always a pleasurable gift to have a glimpse of these other worlds. While in the lucid dream, this man had made an interesting observation. He said, "I was told that I could return home and bring two gifts from Earth with me." I pondered this statement and came to the following conclusion. He was being told metaphorically that he could return with two human experiences to share with his people on this other planet. It's uplifting that we mere humans are reminded of the fact that we have something unique in our makeup that other life-forms seem to be interested in exploring. For this man, it left him not only with a feeling of euphoria but also a longing to return "home."

If lucid dreaming is something that you want to explore, go for it. However, to prepare yourself for this type of dreaming you must do some homework. You must be fully aware of *who you are* during your waking state. A balancing of body, mind, and spirit is an absolute must.

You may think you're conscious of your everyday actions, but you're not. You have to see *outside* of yourself in order to *see* yourself. Just like in the visualization of your theater with you as the audience watching yourself perform, you have to be an observer watching another aspect of yourself from a different perspective. The current television program *Unforgettable* provides a good demonstration of this "outside-the-body" consciousness. The female lead has an unforgettable memory. She's one of those people who can recall every minute detail of a prior event. During the drama's story arc her "spirit" can return and see itsy-bitsy details that she wasn't conscious of when first experiencing the action. This is what you need to work for. No matter what you are doing, whether it's driving your car, washing dishes, or enjoying a good cup of coffee at your favorite café, *observe every single, little detail.*

Driving? Don't just sit and wait for the traffic light to turn. Really *look at the traffic light as a significant energy-form.* See its individual colors and the energy it's emitting. The red isn't just red. It's as intense and fathomless as a ruby gem. The yellow or orange is as bright as the setting sun, and the emerald green is as rich as the meadows of Ireland.

Washing dishes? Feel the warmth of the soothing water encircling your hands. Smell the favorite scent of your dish soap. Envision the sound of a cascading waterfall as you run the tap water to rinse a dish.

Sure, you enjoy the smell of coffee saturating your favorite coffee shop, but are you really conscious of the hum of voices in the café? Does the sound remind you of an orchestra warming up before playing? Do you feel the hardness of the café's seat as your body conforms to its shape? In other words, *be aware of your existence.*

If you can achieve this state of awareness by other means, such as yoga or chanting mantras, then by all means do so. Whatever it takes for you to achieve balance and detachment is fine. If you believe that an hour-long jog along a familiar route makes you feel good, take it one step further. Don't just concentrate on how many miles you have run. Be aware of the scenery that flashes past your vision. Smell the air whooshing past your body and listen to the rapid thumping of your sneakers as they bounce off the concrete or dirt road. Think you feel balanced after your morning jog? You've experienced nothing until you've felt the complete balancing of the whole you.

To be able to experience lucid dreaming takes dili-gence that will pay off a thousandfold in your over all sense of well-being. Even if you're performing a routine task at work or fixing the kids' lunches before they take off to school, *be fully into the process*. The book *Miracle of Mindfulness* by the Vietnamese Nobel Peace Prize recipi-ent Thich Nhat Hanh is an excellent resource for being completely aware 24/7. If you're consciously mindful during the waking state, you will be mindful during your dreams. All you need to do is be diligent and practice. Self-discipline is a must.

If staying focused is difficult for you to do, try a specific meditation that has a central image for you to latch onto until you have your thoughts under control. For example, during my reincarnation workshops, I use a certain meditation to allow attendees to "enter" their past lives. I start with having them visualize a rosebud and experience it bloom, using all the senses to smell, feel, taste, etc., as well as seeing it unfold. The image can be anything as long as it holds your focus. This may take some time to accomplish, as when trying it, you'll realize just how much your mind wanders from thought to thought—that is, unless you have perfected the art of meditation like a yogi. Before settling down to sleep, spend a few moments taking in slow, deep breaths and relaxing every muscle in your body from the tips of your toes to your eyelids. Whatever thought enters your mind, observe it with dispassion even if it seems to be complete nonsense, then let it go. Remember to breathe rhythmically and slowly as your body relaxes and your thoughts flow by. View each thought with a nonjudg-mental attitude until you succumb to sleep. If a guided meditation tape helps, then play it. I have a friend who plays favorite music to help induce tranquility before dropping off to sleep. It goes without saying that hard rock music wouldn't work!

I can't emphasize enough that during your day you need to get into the habit of being fully conscious of your surroundings and thoughts. Do you think you are always alert and focused? How often have you driven your car along a familiar road that maybe you travel every day, such as the well-known route that takes you to work? Have you gone from point "A" to "B" without being conscious of how you arrived at point "B"? We've all done this as if we've been driving via robotic control. We have not been conscious of our surroundings, even though we've arrived at our destination.

Start thinking of "I Am" in any daily experience that you encounter. Your world is all about *you*. Whatever you experience in the world is yours alone, and nobody else has the same experience as you do. You may try playing a game with any friends/relatives on the same quest for lucid dreaming. Share an event or situation whereby the group is experiencing the same "story." After you've each observed the same event, share your thoughts with each other and note how different each viewpoint is. A good choice would be a movie that you all have seen or a book that you've each read. What will happen? The first result will be that either someone expresses dislike for the movie/book or loves it. That's the most obvious experience. But beyond that you will notice how something in the movie or book will have really impacted one person and maybe someone else doesn't even remembered the scenario.

You can perform this fun exercise with anything you want, such as observing people/situations in a restaurant or people's reactions at a ball game you've attended together. The opportunities are endless. Whenever I go out to eat, I love to people-watch and read their body language. It's even more fun to use my imagination and figure out their story from watching how they act. Try this game with a companion. Note the differences in your individual observations. Take it a step further and look around the restaurant. Don't just see the hustle and bustle of the waitstaff and patrons chatting and eating. Closely observe the decor of the place, the various colors, smells, the aliveness of the atmosphere and vibrant energy. You've already tasted your food, but have you savored its texture? Chew mindfully.

I'm sure that you know the example of the games where in a circle of people one whispers something to one neighbor and this is repeated around the circle until it returns to the source. What happens? By the time the "message" gets back, it's not what you had originally said, is it? That's because everyone hears something different. *Life is all about you and your world and how you view your environment.*

It's the same with dreaming. Your dreams are as unique as the breaths you take. Lucid dreaming is the epitome of your slumbering world because you control the story. All you have to do is really be awake and in the moment of your reality and you're on your way to being awake to the world of lucid dreaming You know you have the senses of touch, sight, smell, sound, and taste, but the best of all senses is your feelings. Don't take any of your senses for granted. Instead utilize them to their full capacity. Enhance your senses in your daily reality so that the enhancement will carry over to the reality of your dream-world.

Learn what time works best for you to dream lucidly. If you know that your alarm clock is going to go off at a certain moment and you'll have to get up to go to work, get into the habit of training your mind to remember your dreams before that preset time. Think about the time that you want to awaken before you drop off to sleep. Your mind will do anything you want if you train it to do so. Personally, if I know that I have to be awake at a certain time, I don't need an alarm clock. When I tell myself that I'll wake up at that time, I will. Over the years I've trained myself to do this because I absolutely hate alarm clocks!

When settling down to sleep, tell yourself that you'll be fully aware that you are dreaming. Continue to keep this thought in mind as you fall asleep and plan to have a lucid dream while in the REM stage before you awaken. During the dream you'll feel as if you're watching a play just as if you were a part of an audience yet at the same time a participant in the story.

Are you asking yourself "What are lucid dreams good for?" Well, a lucid dream can leave the dreamer with such a lightness of Spirit that it's almost the same feeling as if you were completely free of your body. It's better than a great massage, yoga balancing, or even good sex! In the words of Clint Eastwood it can "make my day"!

Astral flying during sleep is also a form of lucid dreaming. Astral flying brings forth the same euphoric state of fulfillment. As was the case in my dream of being out in the Universe, a dream can be both an astral flight and a lucid dream. If nothing else, both are as reenergizing as a long vacation on sunny beaches away from civilization. It's just plain good for your body, mind, and spirit.

Some people use lucid dreaming to assist in healing aspects of their psyche, such as phobias, nightmares, and even physical ailments. Remember the woman who cured herself of breast cancer via her dreams? I'm sure that she was fully aware that she was dreaming when receiving guidance. This healing of Self while asleep is similar to having an NLP (neuro-linguistic programming) session whereby the facilitator plants positive thoughts in your head while you're under hypnosis. You can do this for yourself by concentrating on filling your mind with positive thoughts and a determination to be lucid while you are sleeping. The beauty of lucid dreaming is that it can enhance your overall daily life. It's abundantly clear that it's a great stress reliever!

The world around us is a construction of our individual minds. On a broader scale it's what Carl Jung called "the collective consciousness." Lucid dreaming can give you a peek at this universal consciousness. A lucid dream can be so real that one questions which experience of "reality" is the true one. The movie *Inception* provides a good example of the mind-stretching nature of dream reality.

Recap

Lucid dreaming is the act of *knowing* that you're dreaming and being able to "write" your own "script" while experiencing the dream.

Some folks can automatically dream lucidly, but if you've never had this pleasure, you can learn. All it takes is practice and diligence in living in awareness.

Preparing your mind for this type of dreaming is a necessity. Be lucid in your waking state and your mind will accommodate you while sleeping. Practice makes perfect is the mantra.

Don't expect results if you've got to be up at a certain time in the morning, eaten too much before retiring, or are overtired. Mental preparation is a must.

Lucid dreams can make your day go better. Like astral flying, lucid dreaming will leave you full of a sense of well-being and feeling balanced emotionally, mentally, and physically.

～ 11 ～

Nightmares

Nightmares are not nice. We all would like to have a perfect life, including perfect dreams, but unfortunately human beings are not flawless. And so, as our subconscious is a part of our makeup, nightmares are going to occur. Bad dreams are a product of an unhealthy state of mind and/ or body. From an overindulgence of food, drugs, or alcohol during the daytime hours and especially before retiring all the way to a more serious psychological trauma, they occur because the subconscious is attempting to get you back into balance. Have you ever wondered why we seem to be experiencing on a consistent basis hurricanes, earthquakes, and volcanic eruptions around our world? Sure, natural disasters have been happening since time began, but were they so frequent? According to the experts, our planet is off its axis. *The world is out of balance.* Doesn't it stand to reason that if our mighty unbalanced planet is causing it to have these natural disaster "nightmares," a mere human being can be affected in the same way? It's called cause and effect. A nightmare can even adversely affect your spiritual wellbeing and needs to be handled appropriately.

In the case of a psychological disorder, they can be hard to "cure," and the dreamer definitely needs the help of a professional psychologist or maybe a psychiatrist. Qualified help is a necessity with a mental and/or emotional disease, and it goes without saying that scary dreams are only one aspect of the problem. In a less causative form—as in partying too heavily and/or using drugs, especially prior to going to sleep—a nightmare usually can be analyzed and taken care of by the dreamer. Most of the time, a nightmare of this type will be so scary, that it's enough to stop the dreamer from going down that road again! But, of course, if it's a more serious matter of alcoholism or drug addiction, the person needs knowledgeable help. Regardless of the severity of these "bad dreams," they are certainly not conducive to wakening up in a good frame of mind.

I don't pretend to be an expert in the area of the injured psyches that create nightmarish dreams, so if you want to delve into this aspect more thoroughly, it would be fitting for you to turn to the works of Carl Jung or Sigmund Freud; especially the former. But, not to give my insights into this realm of dreaming would be like licking the icing off a cake and ignoring the cake.

All dreams are made up of the dreamer's psyche, and nightmares are the "shadow side" that may be very deeply rooted. Of what use is a nightmare to a person with that rest-depriving, helpless feeling of sheer fright? Do they have any function to our overall road through life? Is our subconscious still trying to convey messages of help to us? Is it aiding in the healing of the psyche? My personal feeling is that all of the above are true. Everything we experience is geared toward our spiritual growth and physical welfare. And yes, there is a reason that our subconscious brings forth a bad dream. We have to experience all aspects of life. We can't always soak up the sunshine.

There are times when we're going to run into a storm, but that doesn't mean that we have to stay in wet clothing and run the risk of developing pneumonia. We need to examine the scary dream and figure out why it has come to us. What situation in your life is worrying you so much that it's causing nightmares? Examining your feelings during the dream is obvious. You're scared out of your wits right? Look at the main symbol that is causing your distress and what it mean to you. If you still don't understand the nightmare's message after analyzing same, what do you do? Ask for another, more clarifying dream. It goes without saying that you ask *not* to repeat a nightmare scenario!

However, if a nightmare has caused "scarring" of the psyche, I can only repeat that common sense tells us that this type of bad dream *requires a professional counselor*. To clarify the difference, the following story is an account of how a past-life trauma resulted in a present-day nightmare. Past-life "nightmare" situations are always difficult to resolve when the person hasn't a clue where they originated. If you don't know who the bogeyman is, how can you tell him to get lost, right? This type of nightmare has settled into the subconscious leaving scars on the person's psyche. Here again there is still hope of a "cure" as there are professionals who use hypnosis in their healing techniques to help the sufferer. Here is a stark example of this type of nightmare.

Dora (not her real name) came to see me for a past-life reading. A girlfriend accompanied her, and she asked if the companion could stay. Of course, I said she could, as whatever makes the client feel comfortable is that person's prerogative.

Unlike most of my clients' past-life scenarios, this one started before the spirit of Dora incarnated. I saw the entity about to enter the earth plane, and she was very reluctant to do so. Her "Masters" were firmly explaining to Dora that she had to, as she had to resolve terrible fear issues incurred in a previous lifetime which were impeding her spiritual growth.

Without going into all the details of the dream, I saw the young lady in a life during the 1920s. As a child she had been sexually abused by a stepfather. The abuse continued into adulthood, and the girl was beginning to rebel and getting ready to report him to the necessary authorities. Sensing this, the stepfather murdered her. She was walking along a lonely street at night. Her stepfather followed her, pulled her into an alley, and strangled her to death. Not a very pleasant experience to take with you back into the spirit world!

After returning from my "other space" where I see these images, I noted with dismay that Dora was crying. As I tried to comfort her and apologize for revealing such shocking images, she interrupted me. "Don't apologize," Dora said. "All my life I've had nightmares of being killed by someone. I'm so afraid that I won't drive anywhere by myself." Turning to look at her friend, she continued, "that's why my friend is with me." The girlfriend confirmed this confession.

I was relieved to see that a load seemed to have been lifted from Dora's shoulders. Regardless, I gave her the name of a metaphysically oriented psychologist who is a friend and does wonderful therapy with people suffering from past-life traumas. Whether or not Dora followed my advice and sought counseling I'll never know. Unfortunately I rarely see the outcome of a client's life story in relationship with the past-life events I help them recall, but I do feel thankful that she was able to begin the healing by learning the identity of her bogeyman. It was the first step in healing her wounded psyche.

I can only say that if you are having nightmares that appear to come from nowhere familiar, consider that it may be a past trauma that has scarred you and needs resolving by a professional. Knowing where the nightmare originated is the first major step. Brian Weiss's book *Many Lives, Many Masters* is an excellent account of how past-life traumas affect the subconscious.

In a similar incident, a mother told me of a past-life trauma that was affecting her family. While on a visit to Gettysburg, her nine-year-old son wanted to see the site of that famous historical battle. She and her husband wanted to meander around the place so he was allowed to go off alone, with the understanding that he would join them at a specific time. When the boy didn't return to them at the designated time, they went in search of him. They found him sitting and staring like a zombie at the battlefield. After he'd recovered his senses, the worried parents questioned him as to what had happened to him that had caused him such fright. Based on his explanation, it seems he had been thrown into a past-life recall from a time when he had been a participant in that Gettysburg battle. Obviously the reenactment was too traumatic to relive at such a tender age. He was so traumatized that he spent many hours in professional counseling. My own suspicions are that the boy had unconsciously been holding on to these past-life war horrors leading him to feel what we now call PTSD (post-traumatic stress disorder).

My thoughts regarding any bad dream are a mixed bag because there are so many variables. Let's put aside for a moment those dreams that are created by self-indulgence, and take a look at the serious nightmares caused by the wounded psyche. Apart from past-life nightmares, the most obvious and devastating are those suffered by a person with PTSD. This type of psychological disorder has only recently been recognized in soldiers returning from war. Fortunately it is now being treated by qualified doctors. Although there are still gaps in the full treatment of PTSD especially for veterans, improvements have been made since the time of World War II.

Going back as far as World War I, a returning soldier was considered to be "mental" or, even worse, too lazy to "pull himself together" when he suffered from PTSD. In fact, such mental illnesses didn't have a name, except for the catchall phrase of "shell shock" to be treated with "bed rest" or in many cases not even that. The soldier was usually discharged and sent home to his own devices. During WWII the infamous incident of General George Patton slapping the face of a battle-shocked soldier is proof of the lack of understanding in the area of PTSD. During the Korean conflict I had a good friend who was sent there to fight and returned with the personality of a Dr. Jekyll and Mr. Hyde. His war experiences changed him from a sensitive, caring individual to an alcoholic who couldn't hold a job. He never discussed his dreams with me, but I'll bet he didn't sleep well! Of course, at that time there still was very little help for the problem. The POWs of the Vietnam War are an even more drastic example, not to mention those who have returned from the Middle East. Conflicts resulting in wars are a nightmare unto themselves.

So, how does one handle a dream caused from a mental breakdown? Of couse, a sufferer should be receiving care from a licensed doctor, and if this doesn't include support group therapy, it should. But also at the risk of this amateur sounding off with New Age platitudes, the person with PTSD needs all the spiritual support, soul-touching empathy, and yes, unconditional love that they can get from those close to them. Due to the nature of the effects of PTSD, it is very difficult for a loved one to always be there for the sufferer. For the person who is close to someone with PTSD, learning all the ins and outs of this problem and joining a support group for your own well-being would be a wise choice to make. *And don't forget your own dreams.* Asking for help in this situation is definitely warranted. Understanding and helping the dreamer to heal mental scars with patience, understanding, and loving support are an absolute necessity. Like the woman with cancer who was fortunate enough to find a doctor willing to listen to the messages of her dreams, the same is true with these sufferers. Here again, because of the enlightened times we are living in, there are more and more psychiatrists who are also metaphysicians. Find one. Make the best use of his/her skills. In the state I live in now I know of several good, professional counselors who are knowledgeable in this area, and I'm sure that wherever you live this type of expert help can be found.

We can still do more beyond all this, and I would love to see veterans' hospitals provide the services of doctors who combine healing of the *spirit* with that of the mind and body. Healing the wounded spirit is as essential as healing a broken body. The two cannot be separated. I'm a firm believer in the power of prayer, whether this takes the form of the patient's orthodox religious preference, meditation, yoga, mantras—whatever it takes for the person to contact his/her Divinity.

Working with the messages that nightmares bring, combined with professional help, is very important. It's not easy to work through a nightmare of reliving the gut-wrenching experience of killing another human being or the continuous fright of knowing you stand a good chance of being slaughtered. Seeing a comrade with limbs torn apart and dying a painful death is a daily nightmare unto itself, without having the trauma enter your dreams. Nevertheless, as in a "healthy" dream, your subconscious will bend over backward to show you ways to work through the nightmare and regain your balance.

After seeking the help of a professional, the next step to take is to *help yourself*. How do you accomplish this? Change your perspective of your nightmare's story line. A good start is to open your mind to the fact that your "enemy" is also having the same type of nightmare. Seeing the event that has caused the nightmares from the "enemy's" side is a good start. Can anyone believe that the so-called "enemy" that we're in conflict with in other parts of this world is not reliving the horrors of war like any other human being? Each of them is also Spirit having to go through this same trauma. Shifting your focus and seeing the horrors of war from a different angle can be the first tiny, but important step toward healing yourself. You need to become conscious of the fact that you're not the only one in this nightmare. Even though you want to believe that it's someone else's fault for having been the cause of your nightmares, they are no doubt thinking the same thing about you. You're in the same boat together, and there's a need to stop rowing against each other.

Change your perspective from anger to charity, blame to blamelessness. I know this is difficult to accomplish in any bad situation, so try starting with an effort to give up the anger in a sense of withdrawal from the problem as you did earlier with your personal relationships. From there look at the "role" you and the adversary are "playing" and take note of how, gradually, the anger abates. The only one hurt by anger and blame is *yourself*.

I have a good friend who lived through the horrors of WWII in Germany. I lived in England during that terrifying time. We were both too young to know what the killing was all about, but as we were born during this conflict, we had no idea what peaceful coexistence was. We still experienced fear of the enemy invasion and the possibility of being killed by a bomb. One day, as we sat chitchatting, we started to reminisce about our mutual wartime experiences and were laughing at some of the silly stories we were relating to each other. My friend suddenly stopped laughing and with a sober expression said, "Do you realize that we're laughing over these war stories and not so many years ago our fathers were trying to kill each other?" Yes, war is senseless. And, although nightmares are a senseless by-product of such traumas, we can become *sense-less* to them with the right help and attitude.

Begin your healing by practicing detachment. Use the visualization of your "theater" as you watch the "actors" perform from a seat in the "audience." At first, it won't be easy to remain detached for more than a couple of minutes, but with consistent practice you will find that it will become easier, until you reach a point where your detachment turns to curiosity. You will find yourself beginning to observe how well the actors (aspects of you) are performing in their roles. Eventually you'll find yourself directing your own "play" the way you want it to be. You may even find that your "bad dreams" begin to change as the subconscious starts to heal. Even that great playwright Shakespeare wrote comedies as well as tragedies.

There are also the nightmares suffered by troubled teenagers. The incidences of teenage suicide in this country are unacceptable. How many of these children have unknowingly received the help they need through their subconscious dreams, and due to ignorance, that help has been ignored by a parent, school counselor, and the children themselves? Sometimes it's unfortunate that a well-meaning doctor or counselor will prescribe a "quick fix" with too much medication. I have a teenage grandson who suffered from depression. His mother spent thousands of dollars on his care, and of course, he's taken the usual prescribed pills (antidepressants) as well as ongoing counseling. He recently shared a repetitive dream with me in which he is always astral flying. But his flights are not the pleasant experience that astral flying should be. In fact they are bordering on nightmarish scenarios. I'm convinced that the story line of these dreams are the *physical* side effects of the pills that he ingests. His subconscious is attempting to heal his psyche with out-of-body experiences, but the medication is probably so strong it's interfering. Hopefully the day will arrive when it is mandatory for all medical professionals to have to include spiritual counseling in their training. Meanwhile, as with veterans, the teenager needs constant reassurance that he is supported and loved and needs help to unravel the nightmares. As with any dream, you use the same technique of exploring all the symbolism of the nightmare and, if possible, changing the scenario of the dream to a positive outcome. This may be achieved through the suggestions that I've already mentioned.

It's hard to fathom the suffering of Christ on the Cross as with compassion he looked down at his torturers and "loved his enemy." Mind-boggling when you think about this, isn't it? As for more recent history, ask yourself how the Dalai Lama can remain so accepting and loving toward the Chinese nation that ravaged his country and committed atrocities on his people. No one expects you to be a saint, at least not in this life! But you are capable of healing yourself of nightmares with the help of your spirit. Forgiving your "enemy" is a start. Forgiving yourself is harder—but still possible.

Of course, there are the nightmares that occur after someone has received an unexpected and maybe less traumatic life-threatening experience as PTSD or teenage issues. These types of nightmares are sometimes easier to resolve as the person's psyche isn't usually as deeply damaged as the former. Once more, here is a personal example.

In the mid-1960s my family and I were driving through a midwestern state and ran into a tornado— literally. Not having any previous experience with tornados, we didn't know what it was as it rushed toward us until it was too late. Our car was picked up off the road with as little effort as the wind dislodges a leaf from a tree. The car was swirled up and around like Dorothy's house in *The Wizard of Oz*, and eventually we were dropped into a ditch. Apart from broken bones, the family was alive (obviously not our time to leave), and we were rescued from the horror. For about a year after that encounter I had nightmares of the *sound* of that tornado. Some folks say it sounds like a train coming at you, but that's not true. A tornado has a unique sound of its own as folks who have heard it will agree. And that sound would repeat most terrifyingly and persistently in my dreams. When the nightmare occurred, I would force myself to either awaken or turn over to my other side in order to disrupt it. Fortunately, time does heal. I also worked through the nightmares by forcing my mind to control the frightening feelings and shift to calmer, less negative thoughts. This gradually helped my psyche recover. I conditioned myself to view the nightmare with *detachment* as if I was watching the trauma as I would watch a horror movie; telling myself that this was just a "movie" and not "real life." It wasn't easy, but persistence eventually paid off. On awakening after such a nightmare, I would repeat to myself that I was no longer in danger, therefore it wasn't necessary for my subconscious to hold on to the "wound." I would mentally repeat positive affirmations to myself and always remember that "This too shall pass." At a deeper level, I searched for reasons as to why I'd chosen to have this life-threatening experience. Most important, however, I treated my subconscious "inner child" with the kind of tenderness that one would use to comfort a young friend who had fallen and hurt themselves. I changed my *feelings* regarding the experience and pretended that I was watching *The Wizard of Oz*, that is, with fascination and awe but no fear. Slowly but surely these healing techniques helped me process the disturbing event. I do, however, have to admit that I'm in no hurry to visit the Midwest again!

~

In whatever form nightmares appear there is always a "cure" when the unfortunate recipient is able to learn why the subconscious is bringing the dream forth. But don't be like a doctor prescribing aspirin for a chronic headache without first finding out what is causing the pain; dig below the surface of the psyche and use every possible means to root out the cause.

Recap

Nightmares are a product of a state of imbalance in a person—physically, emotionally, or mentally.

Even nightmares are experienced for a reason. The subconscious also needs to be healed, and it can't do this without help from the recipient's conscious world.

For serious "scars" such as PTSD or alcohol and/or drug addiction, professional help is a necessity. Any therapy should also include an analysis of the nightmares.

Soldiers returning from the horrors of war need special help with their nightmarish dreams. They need to have healing of the body (physical), mind (emotional), and last but not least—that which makes them tick—the spirit. They need help to become whole again. Working through the nightmares and changing the perspective of the same is a good start.

Vulnerable teenagers need the same type of understanding and help with nightmares. We have too many teenage suicides in our times, and it takes more than a quick fix with medication to help them. Working with them and showing them how to decipher the dreams that the subconscious is bringing forth are a necessity. Once a nightmare scenario is understood, the healing can begin.

Past-life traumas that reemerge through nightmares are harder to handle. The first step is to find out what trauma had occurred during that "past." Here again, past-life regression with a licensed practitioner, who also is open to metaphysical concepts, is the best way to begin the healing process. Knowing where the nightmare came from is a big step toward healing.

Last but far from least, all nightmares need to be treated with serious respect, and the dreamer needs complete and loving support.

☞ 12 ☜

Exploring the Diversity
of Your Dreams

E very person walks a different road through life and no
two paths are exactly alike, even when they intercept
and mingle. But without exception, there is one life-path
experience that every human being shares. Whether we
are aware of the fact or not, every one of us on this earth
is attempting to walk a road back to their spiritual Self.
It's immaterial as to whether that person is aware of this
or not; one person's "road" may meander in a different
direction than yours, but the destination is the same.
Of course, this also applies to those who don't really
care about religion/spirituality or what they're trying to
accomplish. The person might be that powerful mogul
running a megabillion-dollar company or a homeless
individual living in helpless conditions, but either consciously or unconsciously each one is trying to reach for
"something better." That "something better" that they
seek is their own Divine Grace.

Are you a political bigwig striving to accomplish
an agenda or a "Mother Teresa" of this world? When it
comes down to the nitty-gritty of life, all of humanity is

searching for that original spark that is called by many names. Some people call themselves Christians. Of course, this covers Christianity's many and varied guises. Or they may be an orthodox Jew versus one who never honors the Sabbath. Muslims honor the teachings of Mohammed. Or Buddhism might be your calling or Hinduism—the list goes on and on. Do you stop and think about proclaimed atheists' philosophy? Even these folks are searching for something better. Whatever name we choose to give to the Divine, in our deep subconscious *we remember who we are*, and ever since humankind began its existence on this planet, we have sought to return to our own Divinity. Yet time after time the question is asked, how do we get there? What is that enigmatic "something better" that we seek?

To help in our search for answers we simply need to use the tools that we've been given, such as talents, brains, physical attributes, and so on. We haven't been left to stumble through the dark trying to find our way "home." We've been given many road signs to direct us on our journey, and one of the most powerful tools that we have is our dreams.

Dreams that originate in our subconscious are there to serve us in our everyday decision making. Dreams show us the way when we've taken a wrong turn in the road or warn of danger be it physical, emotional, or mental. Dreams offer guidance so that we can make the right decision when we vacillate and don't know what to do next. They are constantly attempting to steer us on the right path, and even when a trauma causes those frightening nightmares, we are given help to heal the wound. Dreams even assist in overcoming karma whether that "mistake" has originated in a former life or in this one.

All we have to do is to heed them and use the natural tools that we have been given. Yes, the dreams that your subconscious produces are an important factor in your search for your own Truth.

Many generous friends/clients have shared their dreams with me to provide examples of what I've tried to convey to you within these pages. This will be especially helpful to those people who think they never dream. As an outsider looking in, I've given my own interpretation to the following dreams, along with the dreamer's own analysis. However, at this point I can't reiterate enough the fact that only the dreamer can accurately analyze a dream. Still I have found that it does help to discuss it with someone else. An "outsider" can sometimes pick up on something in the dream that you may have missed. Sometimes we are standing too close to a portrait to see the different nuances that the artist has applied. Stepping back from the painting and receiving another person's viewpoint will allow us to observe that subtle light that is filtering through the trees. The person might be pointing out the shadows that surround the image of a face while you realize what the facial expression is really trying to tell you. In other words, having someone's insights may show you something that you have missed. The dreams that have been shared with me, I am also sharing with you. By looking at these various dreams and, more important, the messages that the dreamers have received from them, you'll see from a new perspective what I've been attempting to convey within these pages.

As a reminder to you, I am a "show me" person and therefore feel that giving you evidence of problem solving via a dream's message is far better than your having to take my word for it. I am still that person who needs tangible proof of anything rather than taking it on faith alone. And so, fellow traveler, I feel that you too deserve the same consideration.

Remember the teacher in your school who demonstrated a point by giving an example? Didn't this demonstration stay with you longer than something just written on a blackboard or from a reading assignment? I was lucky to have such a teacher.

At the age of eleven I had a great music teacher who was most definitely a "show me" person. One day she brought to school her own precious set of recordings of that famous composition "Carnival of the Animals" by Camille Saint-Saëns. She spent one whole afternoon playing those records and at the same time discussed the composer's intention when he wrote it and what story the music was conveying. I've never forgotten that teacher. Her method left an indelible imprint with me. Because of her example of "show me" teaching, she instilled an appreciation of music within me that has lasted throughout my life. And so, dear reader, enjoy the following examples of what I call "Music of the Soul."

The following dream/dreamer gives a very good example of attaining balance in one's Life. The dreamer has not just "come to terms" as to his place in our world but has embraced and honored who he is, rather than conforming to what society expects of him. His dream removed any doubts as to this. His awareness is so right on!

Homosexuality and Its Challenges

The dream that had the biggest impact in my life was about twenty years ago, when I was "coming out" and reconciling to the fact that I am gay.

I had told my parents and neither of them reacted very well. While they didn't disown me, both of them said some things that caused me a lot of pain. While it may seem disturbing, this dream immediately brought me a lot of clarity.

In the dream my Mom and I were walking across the beautiful pasture of our ranch. We were walking in a place that was very special to me; a little hill in the back of the pasture. The hill was next to a creek and had wonderful shady trees. There was a patch of wild blackberries covered with delicious fruit. It was where I went when I needed alone time, and I dreamed of building a home there someday.

As I neared my special place, I noticed that my Mom was wearing workboots and carrying a rifle. I realized that she was going to shoot me!

That's when I woke up.

I don't know why the dream involved my favorite, idyllic spot but the dream made sense to me. On a ranch when an animal is sick (and not "valuable" enough for veterinary care), the usual procedure is to take it away from everything and shoot it. We'd usually bury the animal where it died. So, in my dream my Mom was treating me exactly the same as a sick animal. My parents' behavior at that time had to do with their sense of loss and thinking I was irreparably sick. I stopped trying to persuade them otherwise, and when I backed off, our relationship immediately got better.

Although this dream is metaphorical, it's literally telling it "like it is" in the dreamer's everyday life and relationship with his parents. His "home" is the pasture where it's "very special to me," and he dreamed of "building a home there someday." The pasture is his *security* where he wants to build his *home*. But, he hasn't built his home yet. His "home" condition is "unsafe" because of the threat of his parents' disapproval (rifle). At this point in his life he doesn't have a safe home base, *because he is still coming to terms within himself as to who he is.*

Blackberries are a fruit, and fruit is symbolic of that which is needed to nourish the body, mind, and spirit. Interesting that he dreamed of blackberries, as black is the symbol of change. It never ceases to amaze me that dreams don't miss a single detail! Fruit is also indicative of the "fruits of one's labors." In a less flattering light it also can be interpreted that he/she "is a fruit." Does the dreamer still think of himself in such derogatory terms? Dreams don't beat around the bush, and this dreamer, who seems to have it all together at that time in his life, probably still harbored feelings of guilt about himself. Subconsciously he still had ideas implanted in his brain from his upbringing, that suggested that *he also thought of himself as "sick."* Remember that people in dreams can be literal (an actual person in your life) or metaphorical (an aspect of yourself). In this dreamer's story the "mother" was both. Not only did she disapprove of him, but also *subconsciously he disapproved of himself.* Like an itch that you can't get to in order to scratch, he also felt "sick" with feelings that he wasn't as "normal" as his parents expected him to be.

Of course, he got the message of the dream and realized that you can't change another person's way of thinking but you can change your attitude or reactions to them. This is a beautiful example of a dream showing self-awareness and having balance in that state of Self.

Repeated Health Warning via Nightmares

If our subconscious is trying to get our attention in a big way, a dream will be repeated over and over again so that we might realize that this is something that really needs our undivided attention. Here is a case in point. This repeated dream is nightmarish, but as you will see by the dreamer's interpretation, it's attempting to warn the dreamer of emotional and mental stress that is ultimately affecting the dreamer's emotional and physical welfare.

> I had several dreams with my horses in them.
> One dream was very traumatic, but all three had
> trauma in them.
>
> First dream: I am looking out back toward the
> barn. The barn door is bigger than it really is.
> I see all these dead pigs laying all over the barn.
> I go out to get a closer look. A woman comes
> out holding something in her hands. It is a really
> small kitten. She hands it to me and tells me that
> two kittens are still alive. I hold the kitten and
> ask her about my horses. She didn't know. Then
> I can see the dead pig bodies clearer; the red blood
> on them from the massacre. Someone else comes
> out, and I ask about the horses. She says they
> are dead and that one has the head decapitated
> and found away from the rest of the body. I start
> sobbing. Then I walk into a room nearby that
> has turned into a police station so they can catch

whoever did this. I am walking through this room
sobbing loudly and saying "why, why?" or "my
horses, my horses!" A sketch artist is drawing a
man's face who might be the man responsible. I
just keep walking around sobbing loudly.

What aspect of this dream do you think stands out the most? *Feelings*, of course. The whole scenario is about *loss*. The dreamer's feelings are very obvious. She is "sobbing," and her stress is profound. The whole theme of this dream is stressful. She is "looking out back toward the barn." I'm presuming that she's inside her home "looking out." Shouldn't she be *"looking inward"* toward her own "home" (*secure space*)? The barn door space "is bigger than it really is." Does she feel more at home in the barn? Does emotional sustenance come from her animals, especially her horses? The symbol of a horse has many meanings, depending on the rest of the story. The following are a few that come to mind: horsing around or not taking a situation seriously, things/life out of order, metaphysically can be associated with the lower chakras (endocrine glands). Only the dreamer can really be certain of what a horse means to them in life, but in this case, the dreamer's horses are very close to her heart, and the dream is showing her horses as having been killed. Is something within herself in danger of being lost?

And what does she find when she goes outside? There is chaos, tragedy, and blood and death. "Dead pigs' bodies all over the barn." The symbol of a pig immediately brings to mind gluttony, a "pigsty," or someone who is pig-headed. In other words a pig has negative connotations. Yet these pigs are dead, as are her horses, and there is a lot of blood. Horses can also be associated in a metaphysical connotation as "message bringers," but the dreamer sees them as dead—even decapitated! Whatever is going on in her life, she isn't getting the message. Death is predominant. Very heavy-duty stuff. Death represents transition or change. It can be the "death" of old ideas in order to start anew. Think of what spring cleaning entails. A lot of dust is raised and there are tedious visits to the garbage dump—then behold the clean and shiny house! You can actually see out of your windows! Blood is life force itself. Humans cannot exist without the continuous flow of blood within the body. It may be associated with the family dynamic, such as "blood is thicker than water." Could the dreamer be having problems within her family that are causing her pain and/or sorrow? Read on.

A woman gives her a kitten and tells her that two are still alive. Of course, the woman is an aspect of the dreamer herself. A kitten is playful, as innocent as a baby, and needs to be nurtured, fed, and loved. It also grows into an independent cat who has "nine lives." When it jumps from a great height, it lands on its feet without any problem. Two kittens are alive: duality, yin and yang, balance of Self through learning independence, and even a lightening up of her gloom with a sense of playfulness. It's also interesting that she walks into a "police station" seeking the one who had harmed her animals. The police station represents the Laws of the Universe. She is seeking her own safety and control over whatever situation is happening in her life. There has to be order among the chaos.

Dream two:

> I came home and was looking out the window,
> wondering where my horses were. I saw two big
> horses standing there. Over to the right away

from the big horses, I saw Penelope struggling like her legs were caught in barbed wire. Then I see Isabelle lying on the ground looking like she was dead. I yelled "Isabelle!" and she moved but didn't get up like she was caught, too, in some kind of barbed wire. I was going to get my big lunging whip to scare off the big horses so I can go and help my own horses get out of the barbed wire. Then a father and son showed up. They were distracting me from going out. I am not sure if they were trying to give me directions, but if they were, they were not making any sense regarding the situation. It was frustrating. Then my husband showed up, and we started talking about what I was going to do. He seemed to keep questioning me, which was very frustrating to me. (Very upsetting dream about the horses.)

Feelings: Frustration, danger, fear of losing her horses. House: *Looking out* of her window. Once again looking outside of her secure place for answers. Horses: This woman undoubtedly loves her horses, and they are once again being threatened. *She is feeling threatened.* Barbed wire: Obviously, she's entangled in a situation that is causing her emotional stress and entangled in "barbed wire" no less. Ooch! There is that number two again: Duality. Father/Son: Responsibility. Authority taking care of the family. Son looking to the "Father" for direction. When you don't get the message the first time, your dreams (subconscious) will keep on trying until you do! The Father and Son are aspects of this woman who needs to look within herself and utilize those male energies to resolve whatever seems to be threatening in her life. Husband:

How often do wives refer to their husbands as "my other half" or "my better half" or, if not legally married, my "significant other"? The woman is looking to her "husband" (her yin to his yang) for answers, but his questioning of her was "very frustrating to me." *She's questioning her faith in herself as well as the husband.*

Third dream:

> *I am in my kitchen, and I walk into the nook. I look out the window into the sky and it looks really thunderstormy. Suddenly I see lightning and hear thunder really loud. Then I hear a small plane engine close in the sky. Then the plane crashes into the field above our barn. A fire starts right away where the plane crashes. Lower in the pasture I see Isabelle, but she is not close to the fire. I say, "Oh no!" I immediately reach for the phone and call 911. A recording comes on and says to try my call another time. By now the fire has grown closer to the house, and I am worried about my horses. I see Penelope coming out of the smoke and looking scared. The fire is getting so big I can feel the heat in the doorway of the nook. I don't know what to do, especially about the horses. My husband or someone says it's too late. I woke up really scared and didn't want to go back to sleep.*

Wow! Such profound and emotional dreams! She is way out of balance and slipping into a situation that may affect her health and/or emotional and mental well-being. Thunderstorm = An important message regarding your well-being. Airplane/Sky = Lofty ideas but her plane is "crashing." Are ideas that she has about her life/self about to "crash"? Fire = Cleansing and/or it can be a "burning issue" that she needs to resolve. Her husband "or someone" is telling her that it's "too late."

This dreamer is a friend of mine, and I know that she was hospitalized with atrial fibrillation, that is, a fluttering of the heart instead of a steady thump-thump. This causes the blood to not pump correctly around the body. If not taken care of it can lead to congestive heart failure. Metaphysically, spiritual imbalance can lead to physical ailments. Her heart chakra is in trouble.

This is her interpretation of the messages.

The archetypal dream work I am doing is working with trauma and the feelings in the dreams. Some of the aspects in the dreams relate to trauma that I have brought into this life from past lives. Particularly the massacre of the pigs may be the less traumatic reference to a village that was massacred in a past life. Whatever it means, it had so much feeling in it. I thought it was an interesting group of dreams because it had horses in all of them. I also had wolves in a couple of dreams, but they're not as personal to me as horses. Some of the fear may relate to my own health problems, particularly when I learned about my heart issue. My husband and I have had quite a bit of family stress over many years, which we have now removed ourselves from. But am just now feeling the stress going away for the last month after many years of dealing with major dysfunctional people: his son and daughter-in-law. I have some fear because I'm a little afraid of his son, as he is a bully and always blaming others and not taking responsibility for his own actions. They have even tried to hurt our marriage by trying to make my husband feel insecure about me and have tried to turn him against me. It caused a lot of emotional pain. So we are finally taking care of ourselves. It was the stress of this situation that was when I first ended up in the hospital with the atrial flutter. The heart condition wasn't their fault, but the stress exacerbated the condition. A lot of it was up to my husband to make changes; setting boundaries with his family, which he is now finally doing. This has helped my stress level a lot; me realizing that I was carrying a lot of the of the stress and feelings of the situation so he could just tra-la-la all along. Now he has to deal with his own feelings! And I do struggle with wanting answers from without and knowing so much in my head and heart that it has to come from within. I have always had so much anxiety in my life that is related to past lives, extra sensitivity, and not feeling safe. Most people don't know that about me since I hide it pretty well.

She has really worked on herself as is obvious from her interpretation. This is a good example of really listening to your dreams, being aware of the message that they convey, and doing something about the problem. Well done!

Past-Life "Twin" Dreams

I have to say that in all the years I've been analyzing dreams I've never run into two separate individuals having the same, identical dream before. What fun! It is such a validation of the power of collective consciousness.

I am standing on the beach enjoying a beautiful Sunday afternoon. It is summer. The sky is clear blue with puffy white clouds; the sand white and warm beneath my feet. There are families sunning themselves in small groups, eating a picnic lunch and conversing. Children are running around laughing and splashing in the water. The tide is out, the waves calm and rhythmic; the gulls dive and cry, skimming the surface of the sea. It is a warm and wonderful afternoon.

Then, suddenly, the tide goes rushing out. I look up in confusion and all I can see is a huge wave maybe 200 feet high. The water is now black, and it seems to blot out the sun. It feels utterly dark before my feet. People are screaming and running. There is panic everywhere. There is nowhere for me to go, nowhere to run. I am so terrified I cannot move. That's when I woke up in a cold sweat with my heart pounding. It's truly terrifying.

The funny thing is when I told my boyfriend about the dream, he told me that he had had the same one. We were both born and raised in Southern California and believe that a lot of us born there have had previous lives on Atlantis. Hence the reason we share the same dream; we were on the same beach when the disaster struck. It is so vivid and real we believe that it isn't a dream at all but a memory.

As I have said, the dreamer is the one who knows what the dream is telling them. And, as she says. she feels that this is literally a memory of an ancient lifetime on Atlantis.

Very little factual information has been uncovered about this continent underneath the Atlantic Ocean, and we know even less about the Pacific's lost continent of Lemuria. I do realize, however, that along the entire Pacific coastline, major fault lines exist underneath the earth's crust. So, these are my thoughts on this explicit dream that begins with such beauty.

Was this just a "past-life memory" or could it also be a precognitive dream, especially as the boyfriend also had this dream? There have already been predictions by both Edgar Cayce and Nostradamus, to name just two great psychics, concerning the major earth changes that this country will encounter. Personally, I believe that based on recent natural disasters and global warming, we have already begun these predicted changes.

Having already experienced a life on a continent that was destroyed by Mother Nature, the dreamer already knows at a *cellular level* what it's like to be the victim of a tsunami.

Now let's take a look at the metaphorical symbolism of her dream. White: Purity, Unconditional Love. Ocean: This symbolizes the deep unconscious. There are many levels to the subconscious, and dreaming of water, especially the ocean, is touching its spiritual depth of power. It's also your spiritual Truth. Beach: Standing/sitting at the edge of consciousness/truth. Your awareness is between the physical and the spiritual. Sun: Illumination. An earthly manifestation of spiritual light. Sunday: The day of rest and completion after days of toiling.

People are enjoying a picnic: Food for pleasure as well as sustenance. Communion between people that is nurturing as well as pleasurable. This whole dream is a symbol of the dreamer's sense of self-worth and knowing who she is. She is being reminded of a life on a continent that apparently was not only technically more advanced than our present civilization, but also destroyed itself because its people got too big for their boots! Sound familiar? The eternal story of humanity's struggle between the Dark and the Light. Literally and metaphorically the dreamer is standing between two worlds: the past and the future, her spirituality and her humanity.

People's dreams usually have a common thread, even though they cover numerous facets of the individual psyche. The most common type of dream is that in which the dreamer is attempting to connect with their own spiritual Self or a balancing of the spiritual and physical. There is always a lot of psychological teaching with dreams and their symbols, simply because they are emerging from the owner's psyche, which goes beyond the physical. This also applies to dreams that concentrate on health issues; after all, in order to balance oneself we have to balance the whole person, body, mind, and spirit. In her book *She Who Dreams*, Wanda Burch didn't go into detail regarding the emotional and mental "stuff " she was dealing with after she discovered via her dreams that she had breast cancer, but I'm convinced that this was not only a physical disease that she was having to deal with but something deeper in her mental and/or emotional makeup. Like Louis Hay, I'm convinced that physical ailments are a manifestation of our overall lack of balance. A good example is the woman with the repetitive dream about her horses being killed and all the other "disasters" that seemed to be striking at her. She apparently had a preexisting heart condition, but her stressful emotional and mental state caused the fibrillations to kick in. The heart is your "engine" that keeps your body moving. If you overheat your car engine and continue to drive it, eventually it will begin to sputter and quit running. If you don't take care of your own "engine," namely your heart, it will refuse to pump "gas" around the body and finally stop working altogether.

Precognitive/Past-Life Remembrance

The following dreams are a wonderful example of precognitive dreams the dreamer is experiencing. I suspect that they are also past-life remembrances. More important is the fact that she is so fully aware of the significance of her dreams and realizes the power that they can bestow.

> This is a dream telling me of the birth of my grandson. I dreamed I was sitting next to a little boy. We were both in white, old-fashioned clothing. We were seated on a wooden bench at a wooden table, very old and ancient. The bowls we were eating out of were wooden. I was told I would teach my grandson Kabbalah.
>
> In reality when my daughter-in-law became pregnant, a female body was reported. The next doctor visit shifted to a little boy. Before the birth of the little boy I heard the little girl calling for her Momma. She will be born next.
>
> The grandson has birth numbers that equal seven; the same as my birth number total. This

is a spiritual path. The family he is born into
doesn't have a deep spiritual connection. This will
be my work with him as I'm permitted to share.

It is obvious that this person is very much in tune with
her own spirit and uses the same in the way she's been
shown. Her path in life seems to be that of a teacher, and
she knows where she's going because she's been there before.

Her dream that is foretelling the birth of grandchil-
dren seems to me to be more than precognitive. Like
most dreams, this one covers more than just her grandson's birth. A dream isn't a flat picture postcard. It's a
priceless Rembrandt that contains depth, light and shade,
and perspective that gives it a multidimensional reality.
A small but significant point to note is that when this
person emailed her dreams to me, she spelled Cabala in
the ancient form of Kabbalah. When dreaming of a past
lifetime, the dreamer will use the language/spelling of
that timeline, and it will resurface in the conscious brain.
How do I know this? Because whenever I see a client's
past life, I automatically speak of certain countries that
no longer exist. For example, Thailand is Siam; Taiwan is
Formosa; England is Britain, etc., etc.

Once again in this person's dream there is that color
white, which is so pure and the blending of all colors into
Oneness. She feels a sense of the "old and ancient." It's so
"real" that it's as if she's experiencing a memory of a previous lifetime with her grandson. The time and actions
seem to be telling her this fact. She and the boy are eating out of "wooden" bowls at a "wooden" table sitting
on "wooden" benches. Wood seems to be emphasized
in her thoughts. Objects of wood are, of course, made
from trees, and trees are symbolic of a common language

for spiritual ideas. This language brings all people of all beliefs together in communion. The ancient Jewish practice of Cabala is based on mystical lore of certain Jewish sects. It is thought that the Essenes followed the practices of Cabala and, incidentally, their clothing was all white. Was this dreamer an Essene in a former lifetime? According to the Dead Sea Scrolls the inhabitants of Qumran were Essenes. There is at least one theory that during Jesus's life, he spent time at Qumran being tutored by the Essenes. As you probably know, the New Testament of the Christian Bible loses track of Jesus from the age of twelve until the beginning of his ministry. Nothing in the biblical records mentions him from the time that his parents' lost him and found him in the temple, until he began preaching to the people as a young man of thirty-odd years. Where was Jesus during that missing time? There are many theories regarding this lack of documentation of his life.

The Tree of Life is of Cabalistic foundation. She and her grandson are "eating" (nourishment) from the "wooden bowls" or the Tree of Life. The Tree of Life is also known as the Tree of Knowledge. It is the sacred tree connecting all forms of creation and religion. I would suspect that this dreamer is a very old Soul.

Birth Number Seven: Completion, sacred, perfection. There are seven days in a week, seven chakras, seven colors of the rainbow, musical scales, and the human body undergoes cellular changes every seven years. Remember that terrible incident during the 1980s when those astronauts were blown to smithereens as they ascended toward outer space in that ill-fated rocket? There were a total of seven. And, one of them was a "teacher." Accident? As Mr. Scrooge would say, "Bah humbug!"

Another dream this very conscious dreamer shared:

> My sister was leaving her job, which was voter
> elected, by choosing not to run again. She came
> to me in my dream and asked to see my mirror.
> I handed it to her out of my handbag. She looked
> into it and, when returning it, threw it into my
> handbag and it cracked.
>
> Spirit was showing me that my sister was need-
> ing assistance with the loss of identity and didn't
> know how to ask for help. I stepped up my com-
> munications with her and listened a lot. With my
> support she was able to leave the job and find her
> balance and identity in her new role.

Mirror: One's individuality, looking at our own Self.
Handbag: One's identity, personal possessions.

The dreamer is right on the mark in dissecting this
dream. The sister looked into the mirror and didn't like
what she saw, so she threw it into the bag. Her sister's
identity/self-esteem was "shattered." And, the mirror
was "borrowed" from her sister's purse. Was she trying to
gain self-assurance from her sister or is there something
else here that the dreamer needs to know about herself?
Remember that other people in your dream are usually
aspects of *you*, and sometimes they are a dual identity—
both you and the other person.

And here is another shared dream:

> My daughter-in-law came to me in a dream,
> and the song "Motherless Child" was playing.
> I asked Spirit upon rising what that was about.
> Her father was in hospice care on the West

Coast, and she was living on the East Coast.
Her mother's health was not good at this time. I
reached out to her and was able to support her at
this challenging time. Her father has since passed
and her mother is maintaining. The passing was
a huge spiritual lesson for her in looking at the
death of a parent.

Death: Transition, loss of something personal, changes, new ideas, growth, shedding outdated ideas that no longer work for you and taking on the new.

~

These dreams are a great example of not only interpreting your own dreams, but *following through with the advice of the dream.* And, note that the dreamer asks for help when she's having difficulty with the dream symbols. Good for her! After learning of this person's dreams and her response to them, I feel certain that she has been a "teacher" in at least one former life and has returned to teach again. Her dreams are obviously helping to guide her on this path, and she's listening.

Astral Flying?

The following is an excellent example of the individuality of dreams. Doesn't it make sense that as our dreams come forth from our subconsciousness, they adapt to the dreamer's everyday thoughts, beliefs, and living environment? I have a feeling that this dreamer experiences a lot of astral flying during his sleep. He has a business that entails spiritual teaching and the building that houses his business is obviously his "home" (security).

*I have dreams on occasion that have what appears
to be a floating black bedsheet slowly moving (like
a bird would flap its wings) inward toward me
(not scary, just makes for awareness). This only
comes when dark forces are trying to attack our
building. It is like a warning to "stay alert" to this
dark energy of the "dark side." Our Divine Quantum Universe has more power than we could ever
comprehend and no dark power will ever overcome that. There are those in the "old world" who
think they can stop the "light" and new world from
happening . . . when they try to abort this light, I
get the warning—sometimes even a vision (same
as the dream) only in plain sight in the day.*

Black: The unconscious or unknown, change. In this
dreamer's scenario it sounds as if it could represent the
shadow side of Self or something that is feared, although
he says "it wasn't scary." Maybe changes that are not for
the better? Sheet: A covering for one's personal comfort
or can be taken as "covering" a situation or one's true
appearance that is being "covered." Apparently this is a
repetitive dream that the dreamer feels is a warning when
he is about to be threatened by outside forces. Bird: Is he
astral flying without being aware that he is doing so? This
symbol is more often than not a bearer of a message. Is
the dreamer actually the "floating black sheet" that feels
like "a bird flapping its wings"? As the dream seems to be
repeated, I ask the question: Is the dreamer getting all of
the message—or only part of it? Is he astral flying in order
to get to a higher level (awareness) so he can see beyond
the physical horizon? Usually a repetitive dream means
we are not getting the complete message.

Nightmares

I was in an outdoor area with a small group of people, and we were facing an unseen foe. It felt large, bloated, and squishy. I turned my back on it and ducked, pulling a friend with me, and then put up a dome shield to protect us. Then something happened, and suddenly all of my companions were gone. I saw one guy with blood coming out of his mouth, and then I tried to kiss his lips but got blood on my mouth. Then I was in a building being chased by the foe. I kept moving into smaller and smaller rooms, elevator, closet, duct, and I felt trapped, closed in, and surrounded by walls; being squished into a small space.

The dreamer's interpretation:

In my life I have been clearing a lot of stale emotions and working diligently at building a business. I have been learning new healing techniques and battling with the emotions of anger, frustration, and irritation. I have been triggered repeatedly into these emotions, which cause me to overreact and blow up. So cleaning them is a priority for me now.

This person is doing some heavy-duty "spring cleaning" on herself. This is not only obvious in her daily, waking life but even more so in her sleep. The "unseen foe" is that part of herself that she doesn't like: out of control emotions and situations that trigger anger, frustration, and irritation, causing her to "blow up." The foe is bloated (problems blown out of proportion), large (dominant). It's squishy: she feels frustration and anger because *she's not firm in her intentions*. The negative emotions are "squishy," and she's not feeling solidarity in herself. The terrifying, wicked witch of *The Wizard of Oz* was destroyed merely by pouring water over her body. Dorothy's problems melted away when she ceased being afraid. The dreamer can puncture this squishy foe with a pinprick and burst the balloon of fear. She needs to take in a good, deep breath of oxygen and expel the poisonous carbon dioxide. The blood seeping from the person's mouth and getting blood on her own mouth when she tried to kiss him is symbolic of her attempts to heal the wounds in her psyche. She is giving too much of her energy (lifeblood) to the projects she's trying to accomplish in her life. The person's blood is transferred to her own lips, and that person is a guy. I repeat, people in your dreams are almost always aspects of yourself. She is hemorrhaging, and it's her male energy that needs a transfusion. When a child falls and grazes a knee, an adult will comfort the child by kissing the hurt better, but the wounds also have to be cleansed with the right antiseptic and protected with a bandage to aid in the healing. She could also be "bleeding from the mouth" through her speech. Is she saying things out of anger, frustration, and fear that she wishes she hadn't said? Trying to run away from the problem is just a trap. Luckily this dreamer has got the message, and she's working on healing herself of her emotional bugaboos.

$\sim$

From these few examples of the various types of dreams, I'm sure you get the general idea of the importance of listening to your subconscious and learning from its advice. Your dreams are your *Truth-Teller*. They help to keep your life in *balance* so that you may accomplish your *intentions*. Sometimes it may seem that your dreams are nonsensical and way out in left field, but it isn't your dreams that are: it's *you* that may not be on the right track—or as I've said earlier, your stomach could be trying to digest junk food that you've eaten before going to bed! You'll know the difference. All that your dream is doing is mirroring your own Self.

You are as responsible for your subconscious thoughts, as you are your conscience. The difference is that the subconscious brings light to that which you are trying to stuff away in a dark closet, aspects in your life that you're not wanting to look at in the "light of day." This is especially true if it's a past-life dream that is having a negative influence on your present life, and you are reluctant to acknowledge it. Of course, as in the case of the woman with her grandson, teaching him Cabala, a dream may unlatch the door to something pleasant and significant. At a cellular level you may already know this and just have to be reminded.

Some Further Interpretations

I wish I could analyze all the excellent dreams that people have shared with me, but this book would be almost as big as *War and Peace* if I did! However, I will share tidbits with you but won't analyze them. I'll leave that to you. Try it, you'll like it!

The dreams and the dreamers' interpretations are so insightful. I suggest you exercise your brain as if you were solving a murder before you come to the end of a good mystery story. To begin your exploration, how about rereading the dreams that I've shared with you and see where *your* interpretations take you? If you enjoy a good jigsaw puzzle or crossword, or can hardly wait to see the next episode of a good TV drama, you will enjoy this challenge. And the most important aspect of this "game" is that you are expanding your own psychic awareness.

Envision yourself taking a journey and you're driving on automatic—except that your car is taking you to a place that you've never been to before this. The road ahead is rising steeply. Aren't you curious to get to the top of that hill and see what greets you over the other side? Of course you are! Go ahead and expand your horizons!

One dreamer was vacillating as to whether or not she should sell her home. She says: *"I am trying to decide if it's time to sell my home. As I am not happy here and no longer feel it's a good fit."*

The dream she had was full of the symbols of "wild cats." These cats were living with her and destroying her environment, but curiously, she wasn't unhappy about this. *"I only remember feeling out of control with these wild cats living with me, trying to keep them separate. And the fact that we were happy."* Cats of course are independent creatures, especially those in the "wild." My pet cat owns me for heaven's sake, I don't own her!

I'll leave it to you, dear reader, to figure out what this dreamer's "wild cats" represent in her life. Hint: The dreamer couldn't make up her mind regarding what to do about her unhappy environment. Animals are creatures of habit and like their comfort.

> *I was being chased through the city (I don't know what city it was) down side streets by a large bull. . . . I ran into a dead end . . . I had no choice but to turn and face the bull.*

Lo and behold, what happened next?

The bull stopped and looked at me with love in its eyes and came up and licked me in the face.

Hint: A bull can mean many things in dream analysis, and so you have to take in the whole scenario of the story. Was she being "bullheaded" about a situation in her life? Why was the bull "licking her in the face" and showing her love? Have fun with that snippet.

All my life I've had a repetitive dream that I was crawling through narrow passages and the passages kept getting narrower and narrower. There was an elevator at the end of the passages that I was trying to get to, but couldn't.

Hint: This person happens to be my friend of forty-plus years, and because of her personality and the dynamics within her family, I know what this repetitive dream is telling her. She does too! But I confess in reality she's reluctant to reach the elevator and the dream keeps repeating. What do you think?

I cannot end this chapter without sharing with you one more dream. This dream really needs no interpretation as it's so simple and a wonderful reminder to everyone as to who we are and where we came from.

Truth of Life

In the dream I was seated at a desk in a classroom. At the blackboard was a master teacher that I recognized, and he was pointing to some

words written on the board with a thin pointer
stick about three inches long. He paused on each
word. I knew he was wanting them to stick in my
mind so I wouldn't forget them. I can still pic-
ture the words that were on the board, "Love is all
there is." It seemed like he went over the sentence
several times. I knew it was really important for
me to remember and connect with these words. It
then felt like Spirit woke me up so I would carry
these words through my conscious mind.

This dream has made a lasting impression on me
and I'm grateful for the message because I know
it is true. When I get to the other side and I am
asked what I learned in this lifetime, this is what I
will say because it is indeed what I have learned.

On that note I will close this chapter. 'Nuff said.

Recap

Everyone on this earth is attempting to return to their own Divinity. It doesn't matter what religious belief you follow or if you're a nonbeliever in a Divine Being; sub-consciously or consciously we are all reaching for the same goal.

We all have "tools" to utilize throughout our life. Some tools are obvious, such as a gift we may have, or a professional skill. But we have many unseen tools, and dreams are one of the most useful of these in our existence.

The intent of dreaming is to make the dreamer aware of what is happening in their everyday life. They vary in type, content, and emotions, according to the activity that is happening with the dreamer's physical, emotional, and mental state. Most important is the fact that dreams will bend over backward to give you the correct advice in any given situation. Dreams are your own personal Truth-Tellers.

The variety of dream types are as multidimensional as a sky full of stars. And no matter how many helpful interpretations you might receive from well-meaning people, when it gets down to the nitty-gritty, only the dreamer can pick out that one star that pertains to their life.

⇒ 13 ⇐

Deciphering the Clues

I t's not my intention to turn this book into a dictionary of dream interpretations. You have access to loads
of dream dictionaries if this is your desire. But I feel that
giving you a few of the most common symbols and some
examples of how to look for clues in a symbol will make
it easier for you to understand your dreams. If you know
how to start with A, then continue on to B, and so forth,
deciphering the symbols will be as easy as learning your
ABCs. However, please keep in mind that the common
symbols I'm going to give you are generalized and, as
always, need to be adapted to your own personal story.
Once again, I emphasize that your feelings during the
dream are of number-one importance. Consequently, the
same symbol can be an ominous portent or a promise of
a joyful occurrence. It all depends on the dream's story
and *feelings*.

CAR: I've already talked about the fact that a car is a
representation of your body, your transportation through
life, and dreams concerning you car need your undivided
attention. Most commonly during a dream, the car is your
own personal vehicle and you are the driver. I've covered this situation pretty thoroughly previously. Pretty

straightforward, right? You are the one who is "steering" the car (control), and whatever is happening with the car is happening to your health and/or mental, emotional well-being. But what if it's somebody else's car you are driving? Ah! Are you trying to be responsible for someone else's life? Then again, maybe you are a passenger in your car and allowing someone else to drive. Are you allowing another person to control your life? Remember the story of Joan? Do you need to take back control in some area of your body, mind, or spirit? Whatever is happening within the car is happening to you.

But what if you drive a pick-up truck or during the day your job is driving a big semi whereby you spend more hours behind the wheel than you do any other transportation? As in the story of the engine driver, your subconscious will accommodate you in the simplest possible way so that you can understand its message. A car will be replaced with whatever means of transportation you utilize the most in your daily life.

SHIP: A ship can also be symbolic of your journey through life. For example, in recent times I have had a repetitive dream of being on a ship and getting ready to disembark. But I'm usually hurriedly packing my suitcases and not prepared to leave, checking whether I might have left something behind. This dream is a very clear message to me. I am on that downward slope in age when I have more years behind me than I do in the future. Like most senior citizens, I'm becoming curious as to what I'm going to experience when I get to the "other side" and almost eager to find out. This ship is my spiritual journey, but I'm not ready to "disembark" from this earth plane yet. In other words, I'm not ready to jump ship and run the risk of leaving "baggage" behind!

Unless your profession is that of a naval captain, dreaming of a ship can also have different connotations. It can literally be telling you that you are about to take a trip. Metaphorically it is usually (as in my related dream) your own life journey, and naturally the story line will tell you what that journey entails. Are you running into a storm, or is your journey going to be smooth sailing? Are you taking a pleasurable vacation cruise or are you getting "seasick"?

It's interesting to note that the ancient Egyptians and the Norse sent their departed into the afterlife via a boat. Did our ancestors know something that we don't?

WATER: In any dream water in all its forms is associated with the Source of Life. Whether it is a mighty ocean or a trickling stream, water is your spiritual source, your power, your inner strength. Water represents the Meaning of Life. As always, look at the plot, analyze your feelings, and then take each detail of the dream from that point forward. What is happening to you in your present everyday life? Are you becoming more aware of your own spirituality, or do you feel spiritually threatened? In other words, are doors opening up for you, so that your life is going "swimmingly," or do you feel "out of your depth" in a situation? Do you feel safe in the water and enjoy its buoyancy, or are you flailing and in need of a life jacket? I'm sure you get the point. Symbols are really quite simple to decipher if you also look at all angles of the story line in conjunction with what a symbol means to you.

ANIMALS: Although humans are considered to be the most superior of the animal species, I personally feel that our four-legged relatives are much smarter than we are! An animal represents that sixth-sense thinking that we humans rarely use, which is a pity. In general, any dream of an animal represents your own gut instincts and your most hidden emotions. Your feelings about a certain animal that enters your dreams are naturally important.

If you have a dog or a cat, have you ever noticed that they will pick up a sound long before you do? If you've ever had the bad luck to be in a hurricane, or any type of natural disaster, isn't your pet usually the first to find safety? During World War II, an aunt had a collie that I absolutely loved because he was not only loving, but very smart. Whenever air-raid sirens blasted their warning of enemy bombers, he was the first one to rush to the air-raid shelter! His act was not one of cowardice but self-preservation. How does a police dog sniff out drugs hidden in a suitcase? Sure they've been trained, but can a human being be trained to do the same? I know I couldn't. I wouldn't know the difference between a packet of cocaine and a bag of sugar! My cat can hear someone coming along my driveway long before I do—and hurries to the door to see who it is. Apart from the fact that she's very nosy, she's using a sense that most of us don't bother to use. If I've been out and am turning the key in the lock of the door, it's a guarantee that she's standing, waiting as close as possible to the door, and I am sure she was there before she heard the click of the key.

Take a good look at the animal in your dream and how you react to it. In waking life are you afraid of this particular animal or do you gravitate to it? Is your dream telling you to beware of a possible negative situation that is about to happen in your life? Maybe the animal is warm and cuddly, and you are being given a message that leaves you feeling a sense of comfort and well-being. On the other hand, are your gut instincts trying to warn you of a possible situation that will impact you negatively? At the opposite end of the spectrum you could be about to receive an unexpected, pleasant surprise.

Most dreams that feature animals have distinctive traits that relate to what is going on in your life at that present time. Look at the animal and see for yourself. For example, most people automatically think of a fox as being a sly creature, as in "sly as a fox." If we think of a sheep, don't we think of "follows like a sheep"? A dog usually represents loyalty, and so on, and so on. I'm not afraid of monkeys, but I don't like having a "monkey on my back" as related in my dream of one clinging to my back. What could be more explicit than that? Whatever your feelings are concerning an animal in your dream is what's important to you.

CHURCH: Primarily this symbol is an indication of your religious beliefs, your own reaction to a certain faith. It may be an ingrained, childhood belief in a particular religion and therefore represents your own spiritual foundation. A church is your Higher Self, the whole person of body, mind, and spirit. The condition of the church is important in the message your subconscious is attempting to impart. Is the church an old, Gothic cathedral or a shining temple as opposed to crumbling old ruins? Is it an ancient, medieval structure in contrast to a recently built chapel? Are you awed and maybe intimidated by the size and strength of the building as you see it in your dream? Do you feel comfortable in that small, modern structure that brings you solace in your waking life? *Are you overwhelmed by the presence of your own Higher Consciousness? Do you feel secure in your own worthiness?*

CROSS: To most Christians this is a symbol of Jesus's crucifixion, suffering, surrender, "dying for humanity's sins." But you have to realize that this form of torture was utilized by the Romans long before Christ made his appearance. And so, regardless of your basic religion, dreaming of a cross remains the same for anyone, including an agnostic. The basic concept still applies without the association to Christ's crucifixion, but at an even deeper level of human behavior. A cross signifies man's inhumanity toward his fellow man. There is a sense of betrayal, cruelty, shock, and acceptance of the inevitable in dreaming of a cross. You could also be "crucifying" yourself in an area of your life. Once again, it's *your* dream and so what does that cross mean to you within the story?

HOUSE: As with car symbolism, a house is your personal structure, your surroundings. Each room is indicative of what you are dealing with in your waking life. For example, the kitchen is where you find nourishment, physical satisfaction. Looking in your refrigerator? What are you looking for that will replenish your sense of well-being? Are you in need of physical nourishment or emotional/mental stimulation? If you're in the bathroom are you "cleansing" yourself of a situation in your life that is making you feel dirty? The basement is your "shadow self," your grounding to earth (first chakra), or your most basic thoughts and/or reactions to a situation. It could also be your "storage room" where you store your past memories (from a past life as well as the present one). The attic is your Higher Consciousness or self-awareness. Is your home untidy and in need of attention or maybe so clean that you can eat of the floor? Is the house a wonderful, expensive edifice that shows a magnificent view through floor-to-ceiling windows or do you prefer a dark, safe cave that protects you from any outside marauders? As always, the details of the dream need to be considered in order of importance to you. A house is your personal security blanket. And, as in the dream related by the man who had a building that was home to his spiritual/metaphysical business, your "house" is always the place that in reality feels secure to you.

MOUNTAIN: Once again, your dream is taking you to your Higher Consciousness. It may indicate spiritual development and what you are doing on the mountain is telling you what you need to do to reach your goal. The dream I related of climbing the mountain via a rough path instead of a smooth one is an example of this situation. If you are struggling up the mountain instead of using an easier path, you are trying too hard in a situation. Relax! Enjoy the journey. Pause and look at the expansive view. It's fantastic! Reaching the top of the mountain, whether materialistically or spiritually, isn't the goal. The only goal in life is to reach your own Self-Realization. Be in the now and savor the journey. Unconditionally love yourself and everything else will fall naturally into place. If you are standing at the bottom of the mountain and admiring its awesome strength and grandeur, lucky you! You are about to climb to the next level of your life.

COLORS: Every color of the rainbow has a different meaning. Much depends on your personal likes or dislikes. In general, dreams of a particular color are symbolic of our emotions, our state of mind at the time we are dreaming. White and black have distinctive meanings. Take the story of the woman who dreamed of the Sandy Hook school tragedy. The whole dream was full of white images—namely Purity. It also mirrors the spiritual Self, innocence, virginal.

Black isn't always a symbol of the "Grim Reaper" as the woman who was having a hard time accepting her mother's imminent death feared it to be. It's main objective is to denote change, mystery, the deep unconscious rather than doom and gloom. Black is the masculine/feminine consciousness or the unknown.

Colors are representative of our own feelings and emotions at any given time. How often have you searched through your closet for something to wear and without too much thought, gravitated to a certain garment because of its color? Taking this thought one step further, after you've arrived at your destination, such as work, have you ever noticed that most of your coworkers are wearing the same color? I have. I regularly attend a gym and have been surprised to see that at least 15 percent of the other folk are wearing a version of the same color as I have chosen. It may be a different shade of orange as in peach or ochre, or purples, lavenders, and plums. It happens so often that I've turned it into a fun game for myself and, on entering the gym room, count the number of people who are wearing the same color as myself. Invariably there are a quarter of the room's total participants who are dressed in the same color. It is reasonable to assume that if colors influence your waking life, they must influence your slumbers and for a good reason.

Sometimes a color may not be easily defined in your dream. If the color is pale and insipid and may even be "smudged," it might be a situation which you are feeling uncertain of in your life. Take the color in the context of how you feel about it. Is it your favorite color or one that you can't abide? Is there too much of a "gray" area in a decision that you need to make. Are you in a "blue mood" or "green" with envy? I'm sure you get the picture.

My mother always, without deviation, wore black when she was working alongside my father in their pub serving customers at the bar. Looking back to my childhood memories of her, I realize that when she was working she was always pleasant and chatted with the customers, but never joked with them or acted too familiar. She kept her true self to herself and only showed that part of her personality that her customers needed and wanted to see. A part of her was kept hidden. When she wasn't working and wearing her more colorful clothes, she was more relaxed and more outgoing. She had shed her mask of mystery.

Hopefully, these few common symbols will start you on the road toward deciphering your dreams. Make a game of building your own personal list of symbols and see how they mirror your own personality. There's no doubt in my mind that you'll get to know yourself more thoroughly in the process.

Recap

Learning to decipher dream symbols is as easy as learning your ABCs. But, you do have to start with A and take one step at a time. Always start with your feelings and move on from there.

There are generally several, more common symbols we all encounter when dreaming, but always remember that the meaning of one symbol for one person can have an entirely different connotation for you. This is why it's important to analyze the story in relationship to what is happening in your life.

Developing your own symbols is not only more gratifying, but it's also an excellent course in self-analysis.

Summary

Now that you've digested the information within these pages, my hope is that not only have you learned that you really do dream, but have a deeper understanding of your dreams and how they work to help you. Hopefully you will not only recall your dreams but know how to read their messages. If you have gained valuable insights to the unique workings of your subconscious, then my intent has been accomplished. Your dream-world is a part of your Wholeness. It is an invaluable gift. You should now be able to read your dream "stories" and from those stories, know how to guide your everyday living and either avoid life's hard knocks or soften the blow when the going gets tough.

Apart from the knowledge you may have gained about yourself, you'll find that it's usually downright fun to experience this other world. Of course, nightmares aren't fun— but we've already gone over the value of nightmares and their healing properties. Looking beyond the bad dream and learning the answer is vital to your overall well-being.

And, don't forget, even if you don't remember dreaming, your subconscious is working while you are sleeping and still influencing your conscious decisions during the day. The manifestations of the subconscious are still there to assist you, and with patience and practice, you'll eventually obtain more dream recall and a broader scope of reality. Patience is the key word.

As you progress with your dream recall and interpretation, you will find that on awakening it will sometimes feel as if you still have one foot in that other world; you may feel as if you're straddling a fence. Don't be concerned. This feeling will disappear once you have grown accustomed to your dream-world. The day will come when you'll incorporate your dreams as a part of your life with as much ease as you breathe in and out.

When in a foreign country, isn't it easier to use a local guidebook than having to depend on asking people for directions? This is especially true if you don't understand the country's language. Getting lost is not only a waste of time but extremely frustrating and stressful. Dreams are your guidebook containing maps and places of interest along with road maps that show you how to get to your destination. Your dreams will even show you unexplored, delightful places that you thought never existed as in lucid dreaming or astral flying, or both.

Last but not least, developing your own symbols is a must. Having your own symbols will leave no doubt in your mind as to what the dream is conveying to you, and only you.

In closing I need to emphasize once more that your dream-state is just as important to your overall well-being as the hours that you are awake. As that master of eloquence William Shakespeare said "All the world's a stage, and all men and women merely players." I would add to these thoughts by saying that what goes on behind the scenes of your stage is as necessary to a smooth performance as the play itself. Take care of your "backstage work" (that is, your dreams) and your overall waking performance will be a smash hit!

Suggested Reading

Abraham Lincoln by Carl Sandburg

Autobiography of a Yogi by Paramahansa Yogananda

Dream Images and Symbols by Kevin J. Todeschi

Edgar Cayce On Dreams by Edgar Cayce

A Gift of Prophecy by Jeanne Dixon and Ruth Montgomery

Living Images by Coral Polge

A Man Called Peter by Catherine Marshall

Many Lives, Many Masters by Brian Weiss

Memories, Dreams, Reflections by Carl Jung

The Miracle of Mindfulness by Thich Nhat Hanh

She Who Dreams by Wanda Easter Burch

Understanding Your Dreams by Alice Ann Parker

You Can Heal Your Life by Louise Hay

There are many helpful book out there for the serious student of this subject, but although I enjoy reading the same, my own suggestion is for you to use your own dream experiences and follow your inner guidance.

About the Author

Misty Schultz

Marie Friend lives in the Pacific Northwest, but was born and raised in Great Britain. Her maternal heritage comes from the Welsh Gypsies and anything in her family that others considered paranormal was normal. All her life she's had precognitive dreams and, because of her childhood environment, was an adult before she realized that this wasn't considered normal for everyone.

For over twenty years she has conducted seminars on the subjects of dreams and reincarnation and has made guest appearances on the TV program *AM Northwest* (ABC). Her previous book Star became a popular subject of reincarnation.